MODERN FORMS

To Olga, Mira and Feliks

Nicolas Grospierre

MODERN FORMS

An Expanded Subjective Atlas of
20th-Century Architecture

PRESTEL

MUNICH · LONDON · NEW YORK

Table of contents

Modern Forms

Alona Pardo
Elias Redstone

For me, modernism, and architectural modernism in particular, is the embodiment of one of the greatest ideas in the history of mankind – progress. Alas, the idea failed, but this failure has taken on a certain nobility characteristic of fallen ideals. This moves me considerably on the aesthetic and the ideological level. My works can be received as a form of a critique of modernism, but I must emphasise this is not a critique that comes as a result of reluctance. It is, rather, a contestation, an attempt to demonstrate what had gone wrong. For I can identify with ideas of progress, I believe in them and I long for them.

Nicolas Grospierre

Modern architecture has proved to be an enduring and fascinating subject for Nicolas Grospierre. While photographers in the twentieth century – most notably Lucien Hervé, Ezra Stoller and Julius Shulman – played an important role in creating what would become the popular image of modern architecture, contemporary photographers are now focusing on the remnants of this era to reflect more critically on the legacy of the modern movement. Modern architecture can be seen not just as the physical embodiment of modernist ideology but also, for Grospierre and others, as an expression of both its achievements and its failures to deliver a better world for humankind.

Nicolas Grospierre has been extensively and systematically photographing modern architecture around the world for over a decade, and *Modern Forms: A Subjective Atlas of 20th-Century Architecture* presents an edited selection of images from his extensive archive. At once a reference work and an ongoing personal exploration of modernism, this collection of Grospierre's photographs predominantly covers structures built between 1920 and 1989 in Europe, North and South America, the Middle East and Asia. However, the buildings included here are not categorised by country, date, architect or, indeed, the political regime under which they were built. Instead the photographs constitute a celebration of architectural form, with buildings presented as a continuum of shapes. This sequence represents a shift away from the notion that modern architecture revolved around singular works of greatness, suggesting that it perhaps had a rather more fluid evolution.

Grospierre's criteria for inclusion in this atlas are, as the title suggests, subjective. Some of the buildings are exceptional; others are exceptionally banal. While some iconic buildings are featured, such as the Gateway Arch in Saint Louis and the Eames House in California, the focus is mostly on more unassuming structures. Grospierre is drawn to buildings that were intended for the common good: housing estates, sports facilities, religious buildings, transport infrastructures, hospitals – all buildings intended to improve the lives of ordinary citizens in accordance with the modernist belief that a better world could be built. The present-day realities of these buildings suggest that the modernist project has not always been successful in delivering on its promise.

There is a strong focus on socialist modernism, embodied in buildings such as the Ukrainian Institute of Scientific Research and Development in Kiev and the Institute of Robotics and Technical Cybernetics in Saint Petersburg.

Several buildings in this atlas were the result of, and successfully outlasted, the communist regimes that instigated them, raising questions about whether the underlying ideals of modern architecture can be immune from ideology. At the same time, epochal changes in politics, economics and lifestyles have also resulted in many of the buildings captured by Grospierre now facing dereliction and destruction, or serving different functions: a Soviet children's camp in Crimea that used to host thousands of children each year lies in a state of disrepair; a House of Culture in Estonia is being used as a warehouse for agricultural machinery, while others in Crimea and Lithuania are empty; and an ornate water tower at a balneological hospital has since been demolished when the complex was converted into a water park.

Grospierre dwells on several unfamiliar aspects of post-war modern architecture that speak of some of the disparate forces that have shaped the twentieth century, such as the architectural phenomenon of Polish brutalist churches, the utopian Israeli modernism built on kibbutzim, and the Oscar Niemeyer-designed International Fairgrounds in Tripoli, never completed due to the outbreak of the Lebanese Civil War. All these buildings are photographed in an unpretentious, straightforward style – Grospierre aims to communicate a clear idea of any given building in just one image – and presented on the page with minimal information identifying their use or location, coercing readers into forming their own judgements and responses based on just the facade and general condition of the building. The photography is accompanied by an index at the back of the book with further information. Collated by Grospierre, and informed by extensive research by the Warsaw-based Centrum Architektury, the index offers facts and anecdotes about the featured buildings and serves as an extended resource regarding many of these overlooked examples of modern architecture.

While the book can be read as a valuable addition to the discourse around modern architecture, essentially it functions as an artist's book: a singular project conceived by Grospierre that is both playful and searching. At the heart of this atlas, and Grospierre's wider practice, is a desire to critique the underlying modernist belief that a better world could be built. Through his photography, Grospierre encourages us to do this too.

A Global Montage of Attractions

Martino Stierli

As the twentieth century rapidly fades into the distant past, the formal repertoire it has developed in terms of modern architecture increasingly fills us with wonder and awe. The awareness of historical distance is thus paired with a sense of the exotic – familiar and ubiquitous, yet strange and otherworldly nonetheless. Nicolas Grospierre's "subjective" – and, by necessity, incomplete – atlas of this repertoire, assembled on six continents, speaks to this conundrum. How might we unpack it? Is Grospierre's gaze on modern and modernist architecture indicative of a sense of nostalgia for the "ideological clarity … of the Cold War era", as the curator Dieter Roelstraete has argued, and thus of an "inability to grasp or even look at the present, much less to excavate the future"?[1] Or is this investigation rather to be understood as a productive mining of the ideological content of modernist utopias, in an attempt to reimagine our collectively shared spaces in the here and now? Or, in the words of art historian Claire Bishop, who, like Roelstraete, was not referencing Grospierre specifically, but rather a strand of contemporary art more generally: "Are these revisitations in any way political, a response to the limitations of postmodern eclecticism? Or should they be viewed more critically, as an avoidance of contemporary politics by escaping into nostalgic celebration of the past?"[2]

Wherever one may stand on this question, Grospierre is only one among many prominent contemporary artists working in a number of media who in recent years have turned to recovering modernism's aesthetics – and, by implication, ethics and ideologies. Indeed, Grospierre's photographs find good company in Goshka Macuga's archival research and monumental tapestries, or in the video works by artists such as Amie Siegel or David Maljković, to name just a few prominent examples.[3] It is worth noting that these artists not only work in a variety of media, but that they come from countries that were situated on both sides of the Iron Curtain during the Cold War, the period in which so many (if not all) of the buildings captured in Grospierre's atlas came into existence. We might conclude that this is a generational project, driven from a position of historical posteriority and by an inquiry into how architectural form might signify much more than built exuberance, and embody bold societal and utopian assertions that lent these structures their credibility in the first place.

Modern Forms presents highlights of Grospierre's expansive expeditions to the sites of modernist architectural production across the globe. This volume presents some 200 images of facades and exterior views of buildings of a wide variety of programmes and functions, yet most of them publicly accessible

and erected for the common good.[4] While each of the buildings portrayed is presented as a remarkable structure in its own right, the artist features them as part of a carefully orchestrated sequence, where the end loops back at the beginning. If this speaks to Grospierre's taste for cyclical sequences – he references Jorge Luis Borges's *Library of Babel* as one of his favorite works of literature – it also underscores the artist's understanding that his atlas (and with it, architectural modernism more broadly) is essentially a potentially endlessly expandable yet self-contained entity. The emphasis indeed lies not so much on the individual buildings and their context, of which we learn relatively little, but rather on modernism as a larger, abstract category. While each of the photographs could possibly stand by itself, it is precisely this presentation in the form of a sequence that gives them their deeper meaning and resonance. It is a sequence carefully constructed on formal terms, starting out from circles, discs, and cupolas, moving on to prisms and from there to cubes and so forth, declining the whole arsenal of platonic figures and illustrating Le Corbusier's famous quote that serves as an epigram and prelude to this photographic essay: "Architecture is the learned game, correct and magnificent, of forms assembled in the light." To leaf through this sequence is a quasi-cinematic experience with its very own narrative that twists and turns, constructs intensities and moments of repose, accelerates, climaxes, and slows down again to produce a drama of multiple acts and with a cast of seemingly immobile and inanimate actors that are brought to life by the sheer fact of their propinquity.

That Grospierre calls his project somewhat paradoxically a "subjective atlas" is both telling and consequential. The selection of images of buildings is indeed somewhat arbitrary, given the vast number of similar structures around the world that might have caught Grospierre's attention if he had had a chance to visit. The term of the atlas conversely situates the project both within a scientific and scholarly convention and a specific genre of image-making that is intrinsically linked to the modern project, and particularly to the visual imaginaries in both theoretical thinking and artistic production of the twentieth century. As Benjamin Buchloh has reminded us in his thoughtful interpretation of Gerhard Richter's *Atlas,* this format came into use in the late sixteenth century and was defined as a book that compiles and organises geographical and astronomical knowledge in visual form.[5] In the nineteenth century, the term in German came to increasingly signify "any tabular display of systematised knowledge, so that one could have encountered an atlas in almost all fields of empirical science."[6] While the atlas was thus foremost a representational medium of positivist science, Buchloh further reminds us that the term later on increasingly took on a metaphorical meaning, exemplified Aby Warburg's famous *Mnemosyne Atlas*. Developed in 1928–9 (yet remaining incomplete), the art historian sought to construct an image-based "collective historical memory" that would identify recurring motifs of gesture and bodily expression from antiquity to the Renaissance (the so-called "pathos formulas").

These distinctions are helpful to further articulate Grospierre's own "subjective atlas" in the history of the genre: *Modern Forms* is neither a tabular montage of the simultaneous presentation of images on a single plane (as in the case of *Mnemosyne*), nor is it concerned with the systematic presentation of knowledge as positivist science would have it. Rather, his is a consciously curated selection of images that are presented in a sequential, linear narrative more akin to a cinematic experience, perhaps aligned with Sergei Eisenstein's notion of the "Montage of Abstractions."[7] We may stipulate whether the formal predilections that are evident in Grospierre's atlas are indeed modernist architecture's pathos formulas, and whether it serves, in Buchloh's terms, as a "model of historical memory" for that architectural modernism. And further, to what degree this mnemonic dimension is suited to recall the ethical implications underlying the represented buildings.

The modernism under consideration in these pages is not to be understood as a stylistic denominator, but as a historiographical marker, for the vast majority (if not all) of Grospierre's images show buildings from the second half of the twentieth century, thus affirming the assumption that his project engages architectural production in the bifurcated world order of the Cold War. Exceptions to this chronological timeframe are few and far between, with Max Berg's iconic Centennial Hall in Wroclaw from 1913 and the Southwestern Bell Building in Saint Louis from 1925 by Mauran, Russell & Crowell with I.R. Timlin on the one end of the historical spectrum, and Oscar Niemeyer's 2006 National Museum of the Republic in Brasília on the other. Grospierre's project is further characterised by its inclusion of works both by prominent auteur-architects and little-known or even unknown architects and builders, suggesting a flow of formal ideas that stretches both ends of the high/low divide between Architecture with a capital "A" and its popularised, often anonymous counterparts. *Modern Form*s thus points to the existence of a truly vernacular modernism as much as a modernist vernacular. This vernacular is held together not so much by a shared set of stylistic criteria, as the selection of buildings span from Art Deco and the so-called International Style all the way to brutalism and even hints of postmodernism. Rather, the overwhelming majority of the depicted structures are public in nature and tied to ideals of social progress and egalitarian access to services such as education, health care, transport, or entertainment. Indeed, what many of the buildings in this selection eloquently express is a shared belief in the capacity to transform society according to such ideals, whether through the Welfare State in Western Europe, socialism principles in the East, or the politics of decolonisation and self-determination in recently independent countries in Asia and Africa. Grospierre's selection indicates that modernist architecture was by no means limited to a specific political system or ideology, but instead a global lingua franca for the politics of progress. The sense of historical distance or estrangement that these buildings exude for the contemporary viewer is a consequence of the realisation that these many of these idealistic tenets were plagued by inherent flaws. Nonetheless, Grospierre says he "cannot but be envious of this moment in time when humans, as a civilisation, were firmly believing that tomorrow would be better than today."

The international outlook of Grospierre's project is key to its understanding. The atlas includes buildings from countries in Western, Central, and Eastern Europe, the United States and South America, the Middle East, South and South East Asia, as well as North Africa and Australia; and even though a certain emphasis on Central and Eastern Europe, and in particular Poland (Grospierre's adopted place of living), is noticeable, the project is nonetheless remarkably global in its framing. As a matter of fact, *Modern Forms* serves as a radical proposition that requires a fundamental rethinking of how the dissemination of architectural modernism has traditionally been conceptualised and historicised. According to conventional notions of Eurocentric historiography, modernism was essentially a project that originated in Central and Western Europe and from there was exported across the globe. Grospierre's visual investigation of post-war modernism fundamentally questions this reductionist understanding of history. Modernisms, myths of origin and originality are not in focus, but what matters instead is how the formal repertoire of modernism became a universally accessible architectural language that was applied by architects around the world simultaneously and quasi naturally. Counter to a perceived primacy of the West, *Modern Form* demonstrates the global fluency and fluidity of this idiom; one that architects did not understand as a foreign import, but rather a valid tool for self-expression and even self-determination within a politics of emancipation, often in the service of a larger societal or political vision.

Grospierre's project encapsulates the notion that modernist architecture of the "three worlds" – the capitalist West as much as the communist East and the Non-Aligned Movement in between – had much more in common than conventional developmentalist hierarchies and narratives would have it. Postwar modernism was the result of a highly cosmopolitan and globalised architectural culture that resorted to a common language while at the same time allowing for the expression of local specificities in terms of materiality and iconography. Although, admittedly, the larger sociopolitical context of these buildings can only be guessed from Grospierre's photographs, the index in the back of the book allows the reader to arrive at a basic understanding of when and where and by whom these structures were built, and for what purpose. The proto-cinematic sequence of images is thus complemented by an apparatus of knowledge; a nod to the very origins of the meaning of the atlas.

1. Dieter Roelstraete, "The Way of the Shovel: On the Archaeological Imaginary in Art", *e-flux* 4 (March 2009), see https://www.e-flux.com/journal/04/68582/the-way-of-the-shovel-on-the-archeological-imaginary-in-art/ (accessed 17 May 2021).

2. Claire Bishop, "Modernist Revisitations" (2013), see https://www.fotomuseum.ch/de/series/modernist-revisitations/ (accessed 17 May 2021).

3. Claire Bishop recently worked on a project exploring contemporary artists who are revisiting modernism through their work, see ibid.

4. The artist has dedicated another volume to spectacular modernist interiors, see Nicolas Grospierre, *Modern Spaces: A Subjective Atlas of 20ᵗʰ-Century Interiors* (Munich: Prestel, 2018).

5. See Benjamin Buchloh, "Gerhard Richter's Atlas: The Anomic Archive", *October*, vol. 88 (spring 1999), pp. 117–14; 119.

6. Ibid., pp. 119–22.

7. See Sergei M. Eisenstein, "The Montage of Abstractions" (1923) in *Selected Works, Vol. 1: Writings, 1922–34*, ed. R. Taylor (London: BFI Publishing, 1988), pp. 33–8.

The Monogrammist "NG"

Adam Mazur

Nicolas Grospierre is an artist fascinated by the aesthetics and ideologies of modernism, as expressed through the architecture from this era. He has been photographing modernist buildings since the beginning of the twenty-first century, steadily building an extensive archive that currently includes almost 1,000 images of buildings scattered across the world – many of which have since been destroyed and can now only be seen in photographs. The artist has always had a particular interest in the modernism of the former Soviet bloc, an interest enabled by the fact that Grospierre, a Frenchman born in Switzerland, resides in Warsaw. The Polish capital's convenient location allows him to easily move through and study the former member states of the Warsaw Pact, in search of new, surprising forms.

The first years of the new millennium saw Grospierre create photographic series about specific architectural moments that ended up becoming stand-alone works such as *Hotel Visaginas* (2003), which explored a Lithuanian town – built between 1975 and 1976 to house workers at the nearby Ignalina nuclear plant – slowly becoming deserted after the power station was declared unfit to function. *Hydroklinika* (2005) documented the ornate architecture of the Balneological Hospital of Druskininkai, Lithuania, before it was turned into a water amusement park, and *Lithuanian Bus Stops* (2004) presented a series of brightly coloured, prefabricated shelters built in the 1960s and 1970s. It should be noted that some of the photography from this period has now formed part of this present atlas, *Modern Forms*.

With time, Grospierre's interest shifted from documentary to conceptual photography. He created several photography-based immersive installations, including *The Library* (2006) and *The Bank* (2008), which explored the nature of the institutions after which they were named. Several photographic objects were also realised, consisting of images which had been digitally manipulated. *Korobloki* (2005), for instance, comprises a series of photographs of buildings covered by colourful emalite glass – a system of facade-sheathing developed in the 1950s – reconstructed by Grospierre in a modular manner so that their facades have all the same proportions and the same number of floors, and *W70* (2007) celebrates Poland's most popular prefabricated multi-storey home system from the 1970s.

Over the years, Grospierre's art practice has matured, and his photographs of architecture have become simpler, yet equally powerful documents. "This could almost be called automatic photography, a reflex I had that meant that each time I saw a building that was interesting to me, I pulled out my camera and took a shot," Grospierre says, adding, "Sometimes I used the photographs I took in other works, like in the case of *K-Pool i spółka*, where they became the second part of a project that referenced Rem Koolhaas's concept of an imaginary floating swimming pool."

Grospierre's photographs, used in a purely functional way, or occasionally presented as part of larger exhibitions (such as "The City Which Does Not Exist", 2012, at Cracow's Bunkier Sztuki), became a collection that was increasingly extensive, but which still lacked its own distinguishable shape. While working on his picture album *Open-Ended* in 2012 and 2013, he made his first step towards isolating a collection of photographs that documented twentieth-century modernism. Those architectural photographs were then presented as a part of *A Personal Archive of Modern Architecture* (2013), a project that lay the ground for this present atlas. In 2014, the artist decided to gradually share online his collection of around 800 photographs of buildings, which included many images from the former USSR (Georgia, Lithuania, Ukraine, Crimea, Russia), but also from Lebanon, Israel, the USA, Brazil and, of course, Central Europe and Poland. His Tumblr site, titled *A Subjective Atlas of Modern Architecture*, gained popularity quickly, having built up almost 25,000 followers from around the world at the time of writing. This accumulation of images exemplifies the work of an artist who has long been interested in indefinite collections and complete classifications (see, for example, his work *Typologia* (2011), part of the "Skontrum" group exhibition at Warsaw's National Museum, or the *Kunstkamera* (2009) installation at the Centre for Contemporary Art in Warsaw).

When Grospierre began thinking about how to turn this collection into a book, he noticed an important problem – his images of buildings, which were constantly being reblogged on the internet, were very different from one another. They showed different countries, styles, periods and functions, not to mention the fact that the buildings were the creations of different architects. In addition to that, the photographs had been taken in different seasons and in different lighting conditions, and, of course, they were in different formats (some square, some vertical, some horizontal). "At that point I decided," Grospierre says, "that the key should be strictly formal, it should come from the form of the building, and a sequence of photographs would look like a form gradation. We start from one building and slowly, picture by picture, find subsequent forms." This interest in gradations, clearly visible in this book, recalls other explorations of a single idea, typology or taxonomy that can be found in cycles such as *Oval Offices* (2013), *Lithuanian Bus Stops* and *Żory*, a photograph from the *W70* series. This string of images also brings to mind the way images are often presented on Tumblr and the internet generally, whilst simultaneously giving the impression of going through a flipbook. When leafing through the book we progress through a sort of formal circle – the last picture in the sequence is the same as the first one. In this sense, the crazy atlas of forms is like a globe that spins indefinitely. This notion is strengthened by the first/last image itself: a round, concrete, one-legged canopy. Grospierre has taken such an approach before, putting images in a loop and placing the viewer inside it; this was the case in *The Library*, *TATTARRATTAT* (2010) and *Kunstkamera*. The meaning behind such a course of action can be expressed by the title of one of Grospierre's works, *The Self-Fulfilling Image* (2009), in which placing the story shown in the photograph in a loop is the core concept.

Grospierre's photographs are carefully organised and give the impression of a topographical document. As art critic Łukasz Gorczyca notes, the artist is interested "not so much in the spatial characteristics of the photographed objects as in their iconicity." Iconic for Grospierre does not mean finished and beautiful, or even easily recognisable. As Łukasz Gorczyca writes, "the photographer is not interested in eye-pleasing visual effects in the form of blue skies, surprising highlighted structural elements or the spectacular integration of a mass into a well-kept, natural landscape." Grospierre is a compulsive voyeur of modern ruins and vernacular architecture, which he confronts with classic buildings by Eero Saarinen or Oscar Niemeyer. In that sense, *Modern Forms* is a kind of biographical record, a sequence of intimate encounters with buildings rather than a soulless typology of concrete, glass and steel objects.

As an example, the photograph on the cover of the small edition of the original *Modern Forms* publication, reproduced here on page 33, showing the facade of the House of the Soviets in Kaliningrad, Russia, is a typical Grospierre axial shot that presents the entire building at a ninety-degree angle. The photograph recalls at the same time the tale about the complex history of the place and the meanders of progress. The brutalist building, designed by Yulian L. Shvartsbreim, is large and heavy, its sheer mass being emphasised by the cars parked in front of it and the boy in a sweatshirt and shorts standing next to it. In addition to the scale of the building, the juxtaposition of a dilapidated lower floor and relatively renovated upper floors draws attention. Missing windows, damp patches on the raw concrete and stairs, and the car park indicate that the House of the Soviets is abandoned. The upper part of the skyscraper, painted in a light blue – an optimistic colour – stands out against the grey sky. This is the result of a superficial renovation carried out in 2005 on the occasion of Russian President Vladimir Putin's visit to Kaliningrad, which was celebrating its sixtieth anniversary. Putin could see the central building from street level in his limousine, so the local authorities decided there was no point in renovating the lower part, which was out of the president's sight. Planned as a symbol of Soviet power, the House of the Soviets thus also illustrates the facade transformation of post-communist Russia. To Grospierre, it reminds us of Potemkin villages built by subservient officials so as not to irritate the tsars with the brutal truth about the state of the country. On top of that, Kaliningrad's icon of Soviet modernism is nicknamed "the buried robot" by its inhabitants. The association of concrete bay windows with eyes and mouths is self-explanatory. Nothingness shines through the large concrete surfaces of the dilapidated structure. It seems that everything has come to an end and nothing will ever start again. There is some heroic and icy beauty in the crumbling

House of the Soviets. It is as if a gigantic animal was dying, having come from space to earth on its last journey.

Another name for this structure dominating the city centre is "Prussian's revenge". Deciphering this nickname requires a look into history. Königsberg, which had been part of the Kingdom of Prussia, the German Empire and the Reich since the middle of the seventeenth century, surrendered after a siege of more than two months on 9 April 1945. The Red Army entered the ruined city, which, according to the Potsdam Conference of July 1945, passed under Soviet control. It begins with a name change in honour of Mikhail Kalinin, a Bolshevik apparatchik faithfully serving Stalin, who died in 1946. The Soviet authorities had no plans to rebuild the ruined city. On the contrary, after the expulsion of the German population in 1948, they systematically demolished the remains of the historic urban fabric and built new housing estates. Sovietisation was supposed to erase the memory of Königsberg's German history. However, the ruins of the castle still stood above the canals along which Immanuel Kant strolled, with the castle spire towering at 84.5 metres high. It took a personal decision by Leonid Brezhnev to blow up the medieval castle, considered a symbol of Prussian militarism, and to build the House of the Soviets in its place. The construction never ended, however, due to subsidence problems, as the structure was built on the castle's ruined foundation. After the collapse of the USSR, there were discussions about adapting the Soviet House for commercial purposes, demolishing the impractical structure, or even rebuilding the Teutonic castle. None of the ideas came to fruition, as if everyone was waiting for the next turn of history. "My works can be received as a form of a critique of modernism, but I must emphasise this is not a critique that comes as a result of reluctance," Grospierre writes. "It is, rather, a contestation, an attempt to demonstrate what had gone wrong."

Nicolas Grospierre's atlas of modern forms can be seen in relation to a number of topographical and artistic projects, by artists from Bernd and Hilla Becher to Luis Jacob. But what seems more interesting is reading Grospierre's proposition in the context of the ideas of Aby Warburg, well known to art historians as the author of the *Mnemosyne Atlas*. If Warburg was interested in the seeping of antiquity's art forms into Renaissance and contemporary times, Grospierre has a similar approach to modernity. The artist doesn't use the architecture itself – that would require an absolute decontextualisation of those objects – but images of it and associated ideas. The buildings, reduced to photographs printed in the form of figures on the pages of a book and scaled so as to match each other, not only show the movements of a photographer who travels across continents and countries, but can also function as an illustration of the universalist aspirations and untamed imaginations of modernist architects. The artist's archive, presented in the archaic form of a printed book, brings to mind the movement of a wheel in perpetual motion. The concrete forms, put into a spin every time the book is opened, momentarily break away from topography and allow for the establishment of a new relationship between objects – simultaneously stronger and looser, and all the more intriguing for its purely formal nature. Grospierre also manages to break the monotony of Becher typologies, while escaping the completely arbitrary character of Jacob's collections.

Looked at today, Grospierre's collection of photographs appears as a cohesive whole, even though the pictures were taken intuitively, and not following a preconceived plan. This body of work can be understood in the context of Siegfried Kracauer's theory that photography acts as a "monogram of history". "The last image of a person is that person's actual history," said the *Theory of Film* author. "That history is like a monogram that condenses the name into a single graphic figure which is meaningful as an ornament." In other words,

14

when looking at any given photograph from Grospierre's atlas, we can see a condensed form of the history of twentieth-century modernist architecture, but also – as Grospierre himself noticed – all of the forms that came before and after that one particular image.

This atlas also functions as a flipbook that can be enjoyed like a film carefully cut from various shots or stills. Grospierre's montage of attractions makes the distance between buildings located hundreds or thousands of kilometres apart, created by different architects and for different purposes, disappear. Putting the spotlight on form brings to mind the "madness" of Warburg's collections of Giotto and Ghirlandaio, which don't take into account the influence one artist had on the other and eliminate the chronological order of the history of art. In Grospierre's atlas, instead of airy, ethereal movements of Botticelli's nymphs, or the Bacchic motifs of fifteenth- and sixteenth-century Florentine art, we see the motion of architectural forms, typical of the twentieth century, and easily recognised in today's concrete-, glass- and synthetic-fibre-dominated world.

Warburg's concept of *pathos formulae* from the 1920s – expressed in the emotional gestures and poses found in the paintings he chose for his unfinished magnum opus, *Mnemosyne Atlas* – is nowhere to be found in the architectural objects photographed by Grospierre. While one could mention the "poetry of concrete", the "distinct shapes" or the "symbolism of the details", doing so doesn't change the fact that the modern architecture in Grospierre's atlas is firmly detached from clear emotions and noticeable expression. Even the most bizarre forms, captured by Grospierre in faraway and often exotic locations,

don't speak as clearly as the theorists of *architecture parlante*, Claude-Nicolas Ledoux and Étienne-Louis Boullée, would have wanted them to at the dawn of modernity. The photographic atlas constitutes a particular collection that allows for iconological studies, but its meaning remains unclear (or is perhaps still waiting to be explained). Meanwhile, the artist arranges his pictorial archive in an intuitive manner, creating surreal landscapes. The architectural forms collected by Grospierre and arranged in a *dynamogram* in the shape of a book resemble Warburg's mnemic waves (*mnemische Wellen*), in that they are a flow of visual energy that might be difficult to decode, but that can nevertheless be seen as a logical sequence.

Many pictures from Nicolas Grospierre's atlas show buildings – and therefore modernity – in disrepair. Decaying structures overgrown with grass and shrubbery, sometimes decorated with people who function as mere staffage, resemble eighteenth-century etchings of Roman ruins. They are one of the artist's recurring motifs – in 2008 he was awarded the Golden Lion at the Architecture Biennale in Venice for an exhibition titled "The Afterlife of Buildings" (a joint undertaking with Kobas Laksa, and curated by Grzegorz Piątek and Jarosław Trybuś). While the Venetian exhibition featured futuristic fantasies of the fall of modern architecture by Laksa, *Modern Forms* shows a future that was predicted by modernism, and that has already ended. In other words, the modernity presented in this volume is for Nicolas Grospierre what antiquity was for Renaissance and Enlightenment artists. The curators of documenta 12, Roger M. Buergel and Ruth Noack, posed the question, "Is modernity our antiquity?" Grospierre's atlas gives a clear, affirmative answer.

15

This is a revised and expanded version of a text originally written by Adam Mazur for the first edition of *Modern Forms*.

Architecture is the learned game, correct and magnificent, of forms assembled in the light.

Le Corbusier, *Toward an Architecture*

Bus Stop, Koreiz, Crimea, Russia

Space Museum and Heliport, International Fairgrounds, Tripoli, Lebanon

Organ Console, Stone Mountain Park, Atlanta, Georgia

Cross-City Line Powiśle Station Lower Entrance, Warsaw, Poland

Tehran City Theatre, Tehran, Iran

Aviation Museum, Belgrade, Serbia

Slovak Radio Building, Bratislava, Slovakia

State Government Office, Geelong, Australia

Hotel Onogošt, Nikšić, Montenegro

Ciech Headquarters Building, Warsaw, Poland

Swiss Medical Research Foundation, Geneva, Switzerland

Association of Design Studios Building, Prague, Czech Republic

Trade Union House, Bratislava, Slovakia

ICI House, Melbourne, Australia

Brazilian Insurance Office Building, Brasília, Brazil

House of Soviets, Kaliningrad, Russia

Residential Tower, Saint Petersburg, Russia

Lisbon Palace of Justice, Lisbon, Portugal

Residential Building, Kiev, Ukraine

Housing Estate, Vasilyevsky Island, Saint Petersburg, Russia

Southwestern Bell Building, Saint Louis, Missouri, USA

Manchester Unity Building, Melbourne, Australia

Rosomak Sanatorium, Ustroń-Zawodzie, Poland

Cité Administrative, Lille, France

Silesian Skyscraper, Katowice, Poland

Totem Tower, Paris, France

Stars Housing Estate, Katowice, Poland

Grunwald Square Housing Estate, Wrocław, Poland

"The Corns" Towers, "1000 Years" Housing Estate, Katowice, Poland

Torres Blancas Housing Estate, Madrid, Spain

Banco De Crédito Del Perú, Agencia Miraflores, Lima, Peru

Strahov Tunnel Ventilation Tower, Prague, Czech Republic

Pardo Office Centre, Lima, Peru

51

Blok 5 Housing Estate, Podgorica, Montenegro

Bank of Ayudhya, Bang Rak Branch, Bangkok, Thailand

Izbor Department Store, Bar, Montenegro

State Archive, Warsaw, Poland

House of the Revolution, Bar, Montenegro

Salyut Hotel, Kiev, Ukraine

Balneological Hospital Water Tower, Druskininkai, Lithuania

Palace of Ceremonial Rites and Weddings, Tbilisi, Georgia

CATA House of Culture, Cesis, Latvia

Auksinės Kopos Vacation Home, Šventoji, Lithuania

Balneological Hospital, Druskininkai, Lithuania

VDNKh Main Building, Tbilisi, Georgia

Dubulti Train Station, Jūrmala, Latvia

Theme Building, Los Angeles, California, USA

Angarskyi Pass Trolleybus Stop, E. 105 Highway, Crimea, Russia

Gateway Arch, Saint Louis, Missouri, USA

Birds of Prey Aviary, Sofia Zoo, Sofia, Bulgaria

Church of Our Lady of the Scapular, Pokrzywnica, Poland

Church of Santa María Reina, Lima, Peru

Gate, Iran University of Science and Technology, Tehran, Iran

Sanctuary of the Divine Mercy, Kalisz, Poland

Church of Saint Maximilian Kolbe, Cracow, Poland

Church of Our Lady of the Gate of Dawn, Cracow, Poland

Church of Saint Maximilian Maria Kolbe, Kolnica, Poland

House of Scientists' Creative Work, Katsiveli, Crimea, Russia

Great Ape House, Kansas City Zoo, Missouri, USA

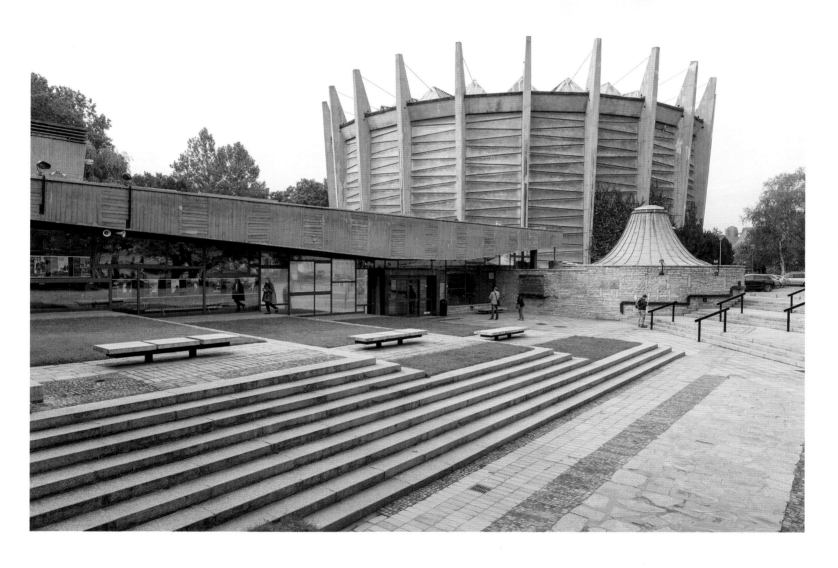

Racławice Panorama Building, Wrocław, Poland

Spanish Cultural Heritage Institute, Madrid, Spain

Institute of Robotics and Technical Cybernetics, Saint Petersburg, Russia

Carillon, Stone Mountain Park, Atlanta, Georgia, USA

Open-air Theatre, Šventoji, Lithuania

Memorial House, Bogetići, Montenegro

Temple of the Community of Christ, Independence, Missouri, USA

Chapel of Thanksgiving, Dallas, Texas, USA

Chamber of Deputies Chapel, Brasília, Brazil

Brighton Municipal Offices, Melbourne, Australia

Orlov Museum of Paleontology, Moscow, Russia

Monash University Religious Centre, Melbourne, Australia

Hoover Dam, Nevada, USA

Nemunas Hotel Concert Hall, Druskininkai, Lithuania

Dining Hall, Donbass Sanatorium, Massandra, Crimea, Russia

Jimmy Carter Presidential Library and Museum, Atlanta, Georgia, USA

Museum of Archaeology, Tbilisi, Georgia

94

Church of Saint Jan Kanty, Cracow, Poland

VDNKh Pavilion no.10, Tbilisi, Georgia

Dining Hall, Kibbutz Sha'ar HaGolan, Israel

Fishing Terminal Canopy, Pucusana, Peru

Bathing Pool, Kaliningrad, Russia

Customs and Firefighting Quarter, International Fairgrounds, Tripoli, Lebanon

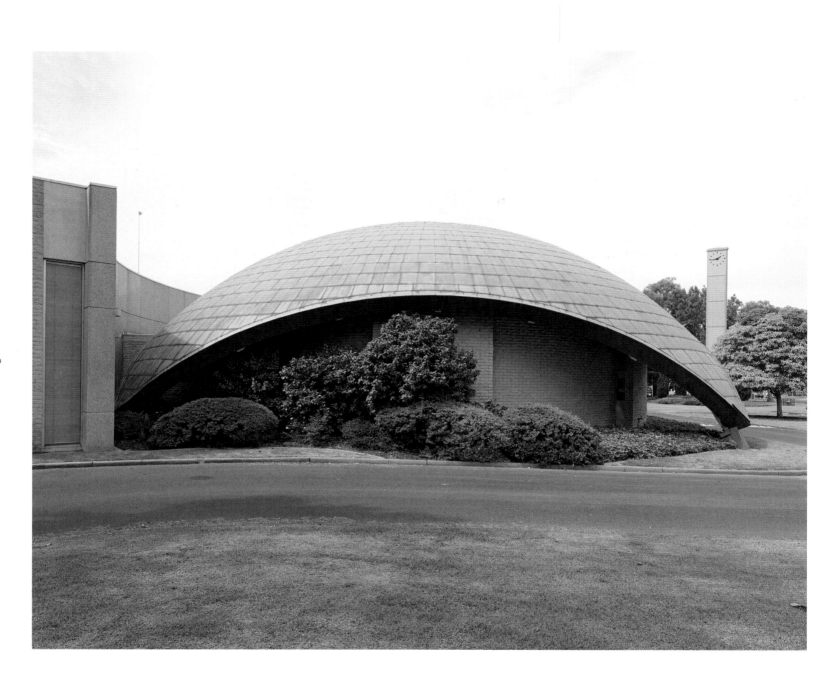

Civic Offices Council Chamber, Altona, Australia

Shine Dome, Canberra, Australia

Sēnīte Restaurant, A2 Highway, near Krustiņi, Latvia

Pol'ana Hotel, Tatranská Javorina, Slovakia

Concert Shell, International Fairgrounds, Tripoli, Lebanon

Gas Station, Marrakech, Morocco

Bus Stop, Lithuania

Bus Stop, Foros, Crimea, Russia

Bus Stop, Partenit, Crimea, Russia

Bus Stop, Lithuania

Dead Sea Museum and Visitor Center, Neve Zohar, Israel

Bus Station, Kupiškis, Lithuania

First Federal Savings and Loan Association Branch, Texarkana, Texas/Arkansas, USA

Palace of Pioneers, Moscow. Russia

Church of Jesus Christ of Latter-day Saints Visitors' Center, Independence, Missouri, USA

Lebanese Pavilion, International Fairgrounds, Tripoli, Lebanon

Palace of Justice, Brasília, Brazil

Tharmaratnam Residence, Colombo, Sri Lanka

Cross-City Line Powiśle Station Upper Entrance, Warsaw, Poland

Cross-City Line Ochota Station, Warsaw Poland

Pride Cleaners, Chicago, Illinois, USA

Roy's Motel and Café, Amboy, California, USA

Church of Our Lady of Fatima, Brasília, Brazil

Church of Jesus the Good Shepherd, Cracow, Poland

Church of the Exaltation of the Holy Cross, Żory-Rój, Poland

Church of Holy Hedwig, Pszczyna, Poland

All Saints Anglican Church, Rosebud, Australia

House of Culture, Kibbutz HaOgen, Israel

Memorial House, Tjentište, Bosnia and Herzegovina

Church of the Lord Jesus the Good Shepherd, Rudy-Rysie, Poland

Strumok Roadside Restaurant, Kiev, Ukraine

House of Culture, Saulkrasti, Latvia

Motel Miljevina, Miljevina, Bosnia and Herzegovina

Church of the Body of Christ, Wrzosowa, Poland

House of Ritual Services, Vilnius, Lithuania

Sutjeska Memorial Monument, Tjentište, Bosnia and Herzegovina

Tancredo Neves Pantheon of Fatherland and Freedom, Brasília, Brazil

Crematorium, Kiev, Ukraine

House of Culture for Youth, Kibbutz Heftziba, Israel

Palace of Weddings, Vilnius, Lithuania

140

Movie Theatre, Valgeranna, Estonia

Daugavkrasti Hotel, Jēkabpils, Latvia

Renaissance Cinema, Daugavpils, Latvia

Archive Building, Atlanta, Georgia, USA

Bank of Manhattan Trust Company, New York, USA

House of Culture, Alupka, Crimea, Russia

Nuclear Power Plant, Ignalina, Lithuania

Universal Store, Uhlove, Crimea, Russia

Silesian Institute of Science, Katowice, Poland

Hilda Melvin and Gerard Furst Library, Mitzpe Ramon, Israel

VDNKh Pavilion no. 7, Tbilisi, Georgia

Russian Academy of Sciences, Moscow, Russia

Pavilion at the Nymphengarten, Karlsruhe, Germany

Bus Station, Kaliningrad, Russia

154

Sports Palace, Frunze Kolkhoz, Crimea, Russia

Latter Day Saints Auditorium, Independence, Missouri, USA

Centennial Hall, Wrocław, Poland

156

Urania Sports Hall, Olsztyn, Poland

Institute of Scientific and Technical Information, Kiev, Ukraine

Spodek Sports Hall, Katowice, Poland

Abandoned Solar Radio Telescope, Crimean Laser Observatory, Katsiveli, Crimea, Russia

Concert Shell, Gdynia, Poland

National Museum of the Republic, Brasília, Brazil

163

Experimental Theatre, International Fairgrounds, Tripoli, Lebanon

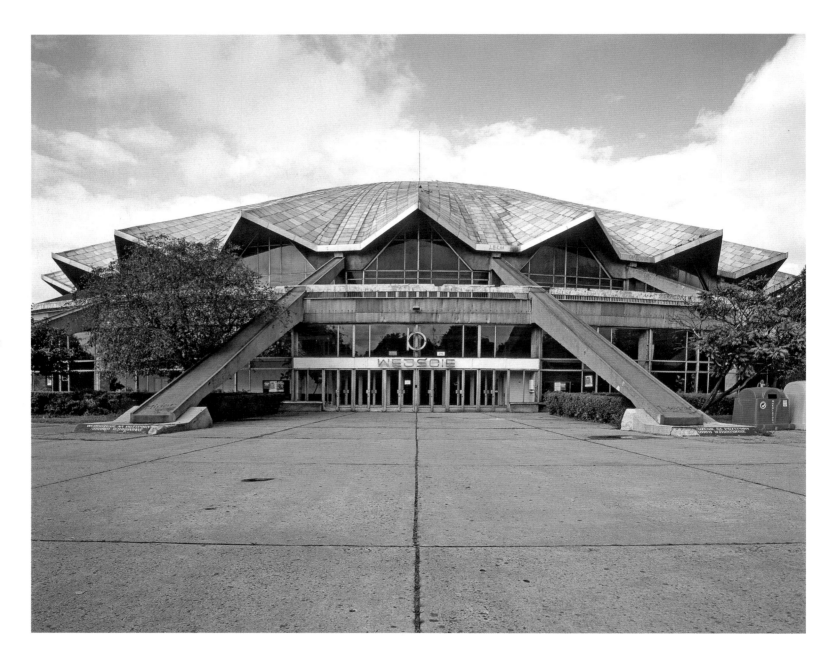

Arena Multi-purpose Hall, Poznań, Poland

Legia Stadium Ticket Booth, Warsaw, Poland

"Rannapere" Retirement Home, Haabneeme, Estonia

Poster Museum, Warsaw, Poland

Watsungwej Printing School, Bangkok, Thailand

Guildhall West Wing, London, UK

VDNKh Pavilion no. 9 "Intra-Trade", Kiev, Ukraine

Municipal House of Sports, Tarnów, Poland

Eames House, Pacific Palisades, California, USA

Yellow Housing Estate, Warsaw, Poland

Banque Lombard Odier & Cie, Geneva, Switzerland

Rector's Office, Nicolaus Copernicus University Campus, Toruń, Poland

Housing Super-Unit, Katowice, Poland

Superquadra South 104, Brasília, Brazil

Hanoi Children's Palace, Hanoi, Vietnam

Parking Lot, Texarkana, Texas/Arkansas, USA

House of Sports and Culture, Former "Linda" Kolkhoz, Võru, Estonia

National Historical Museum, Sofia, Bulgaria

Rowing Club, Warsaw, Poland

VDNKh Pavilion no. 19 "Common Consumption Goods", Kiev, Ukraine

184

Klimatopavilon, Ministry of Internal Affairs Sanatorium, Yevpatoriya, Crimea, Russia

Sunbathing Platform, Central Military Clinical Sanatorium, Alupka, Crimea, Russia

Onogošt Hotel Garden Pavilion, Nikšić, Montenegro

Ministry of Highways, Tbilisi, Georgia

Palace of Culture and Sports of the Ministry of the Interior, Vilnius, Lithuania

House of Culture, Kibbutz Kfar Blum, Israel

Slovak National Archives, Bratislava, Slovakia

Palace of Ritual Services, Pärnu, Estonia

House of Culture, Former "Marytė Melninkaitė" Kolkhoz, Dotnuva, Lithuania

House of Culture, Former "Tamsalu" Kolkhoz, Tamsalu, Estonia

Dining Hall, Kibbutz Mishmar HaNegev, Israel

Tarnovia Hotel, Tarnów, Poland

Trade Union Cultural Centre, Tbilisi, Georgia

Shams Building, Beirut, Lebanon

Slovak National Gallery, Bratislava, Slovakia

199

Równica Sanatorium, Ustroń-Zawodzie, Poland

Pelegrin Hotel, Kupari, Croatia

Colonial Mutual Building, Canberra, Australia

House of Composers' Creative Work, Borjomi, Georgia

College of Liberal Arts and Sciences Building, University of Illinois Campus, Chicago, Illinois, USA

Uni Dufour Building, Geneva, Switzerland

Church of Saint Michael, Karlsruhe, Germany

Municipality Council Building, Essaouira, Morocco

Town Hall, Agadir, Morocco

208

Nightingale Olympic Co. Building, Bangkok, Thailand

Residential Building, Tehran, Iran

Residential Building, Bangkok, Thailand

Hotel Biserna Obala, Čanj, Montenegro

Hotel Medea, Batumi, Georgia

Residential Building, Lima, Peru

214

Hotel Meskheti, Batumi, Georgia

Chorhoz Sanatorium, Kobuleti, Georgia

Dilapidated Hotel, Borjomi, Georgia

Guboja Hotel and Sanatorium, Šventoji, Lithuania

Museum for Contemporary Art, Tehran, Iran

New Students House, Podgorica, Montenegro

El Fath Housing Estate, Essaouira, Morocco

Ramot Polin Housing Estate, Jerusalem, Israel

Lino Swimming Pool, Palanga, Lithuania

Private Villa, Warsaw, Poland

House of Composers' Union, Vilnius, Lithuania

225

Technical School Auditorium, Former "Jäneda" Sovkhoz, Jäneda, Estonia

Bowling Pavilion, Šventoji, Lithuania

Mladost Hotel, Tjentište, Bosnia and Herzegovina

228

"Kormoran" Resort, Olsztynek, Poland

Pyramid, International Fairgrounds, Tripoli, Lebanon

Church of the Immaculate Heart of Our Lady Mary, Czerwonak, Poland

231

Water Slide, Brooklyn, New York, NY, USA

Izbor Department Store, Bar, Montenegro

Okta Centrum, Former "Rapla" Kolkhoz, Rapla, Estonia

Music Pavilion, Borjomi, Georgia

Third Church of Christ, Scientist, Washington, DC, USA

House of Culture Auditorium, Kibbutz Netzer Sereni, Israel

Ben-Gurion Heritage Institute, Midreshet Sde Boker, The Negev, Israel

National Palace of Culture, Sofia, Bulgaria

Interfaith Medical Center, Brooklyn, New York, NY, USA

General Secretariat of the Andean Community, Lima, Peru

High Court of Australia, Canberra, Australia

Rugelis Holiday Complex, Palanga, Lithuania

Lyndon B. Johnson Presidential Library and Museum, Austin, Texas, USA

Niavaran Palace Library, Tehran, Iran

Friends Club and Library, Kibbutz Gazit, Israel

Tel Hazor Archaeological Museum, Kibbutz Ayelet HaShahar, Israel

Fish Market Canopy, Essaouira, Morocco

Gas Station, Ljubljana, Slovenia

Canopy, Olympic Village, Munich, Germany

Coffee Shop, International Fairgrounds, Tripoli, Lebanon

Canopy, Donbass Sanatorium, Massandra, Crimea, Russia

Canopy, Artek Young Pioneers Camp, Hurzuf, Crimea, Russia

Bus Stop, Vinohradnyi, Crimea, Russia

254

Bus Stop, Tulove, Crimea, Russia

See entry on p. 18

Index

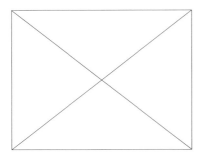

Name, date of photograph

Location

Date of construction
Architect

Other information

Bus Stop, 2012

Koreiz, Crimea, Russia

1970s
architect unknown

Although there were standard designs for bus stops in the USSR, these were often modified by the local craftspeople and were different in each republic. Their authors often remain unknown, although there are two famous creators: Georgian artist Zurab Tsereteli and Belarusian architect Armen Sardarov, who designed over 100 of these structures. [p. 18]

Space Museum and Heliport, 2010

International Fairgrounds, Tripoli, Lebanon
1975 (unfinished)
Oscar Niemeyer

Commissioned in 1962, the Tripoli International Fairgrounds were supposed to serve as a showcase for Lebanon and present a modern vision for the country's development. However, the construction of the fairgrounds was interrupted by the outbreak of the Lebanese Civil War in 1975 and was never completed. [p. 19]

Organ Console, 2013

Stone Mountain Park, Atlanta, Georgia
c. 1964
architect unknown

This structure houses a Schulmerich organ, which is used to play the 732-bell carillon located on a neighbouring island in the park. The carillon was donated by the Coca-Cola Company after being exhibited at the 1964 World's Fair in New York and has been played by Mrs Mabel Sharp for over 30 years.
[p. 20]

Cross-City Line Powiśle Station Lower Entrance, 2004
Warsaw, Poland

1963
Arseniusz Romanowicz,
Piotr Szymaniak

A freestanding paraboloid structure, this engineering solution refers to the work of Felix Candela and Eduardo Catalano from the 1950s. Although the form was considered at the time somewhat arbitrary, the architects justified the mushroom-shaped roof as a way to shelter passengers from the rain while they were queuing to buy train tickets. [p. 21]

Tehran City Theatre, 2015

Tehran, Iran

1972
Ali Sardar Afkhami

[p. 22]

Aviation Museum, 2017

Belgrade, Serbia

1989
Ivan Štraus

Housed in a stunning cantilevered geodesic torus-shaped structure, the museum – which took twenty years to plan and build – holds more than 200 aircrafts. Among them, and most significantly, is the wreckage of the USA's F-117 Nighthawk stealth aircraft shot down during NATO's bombing of Belgrade in March 1999.
[p. 23]

Slovak Radio Building, 2015

Bratislava, Slovakia

1983
Štefan Svetko, Štefan Ďurkovič,
Barnabáš Kissling

Considered as one of the modern
landmarks of Bratislava, this inverted
pyramid's construction started as early
as 1967, to be finished more than
fifteen years later. As it was built at a
time of political relaxation, the architects were allowed to experiment with
advanced construction technologies.
[p. 24]

State Government Office, 2017

Geelong, Australia

1979
Buchan Laird & Bawden

It is fitting that the structure housing
this government office would take the
shape of an inverted pyramid. If the
regular pyramid recalls a Leviathan-
type state, with the leader alone at top,
then the inverted pyramid may be the
image of a democratic regime, with
the government structure (at the bot-
tom) supporting the growing numbers
of citizens (on top). [p. 25]

Hotel Onogošt, 2018

Nikšić, Montenegro

1982
Ivan and Tihomir Štraus

The original building was raised in
the early 1950s. Introducing modern
ways of living in Montenegro, it was
famed to be the only place in Nikšić
where one could dance to jazz music
and enjoy abstract wall mosaics. The
futuristic cantilevered multi-storey
structure was added 30 years later.
[p. 26]

Ciech Headquarters Building, 2010

Warsaw, Poland

1991
architect unknown

While the architect is officially
unknown, the design is attributed to
a group of architects from Czechoslovakia, possibly due to the similarity of
the form to the Slovak radio building.
The building was designed in the
1970s and construction began in
1980. It was finally completed in 1991
and then destroyed in 2011.
[p. 27]

259

Swiss Medical Research Foundation,
2017
Geneva, Switzerland

1976
Jack Vicajee Bertoli

Quasi-officially nicknamed "The
Tulip", because of its shape and
copper-tinted windows, this
cantilevered building owns its up-held
structure to the fact that it was built
on a tiny and sloped plot of land, with
no need – or even possibility – to
make an expansive entrance.
[p. 28]

Association of Design Studios Buildings,
2018
Prague, Czech Republic

1974
Karel Prager, Jiří Kadeřábek

Originally planned as the seat of the
Association of Design Studios, the political change after the Prague Spring
of 1968 had the building serve a different purpose: the Project Institute for
the Construction of Prague. The floating structure refers to Karel Prager's
concept of "vertical city", the studios
being built on bridge structures above
the entrance to the buildings. [p. 29]

Trade Union House, 2015

Bratislava, Slovakia

1980
Ferdinand Konček, Iľja Skoček,
Ľubomír Titl

The contest for the Trade Union
House was announced as early as
1955, but it took almost ten years
of planning and another fifteen of
construction before the building was
finally finished, after going through a
number of alterations.
[p. 30]

ICI House, 2017

Melbourne, Australia

1959
Osborn McCutcheon

With its massive yet minimalist
curtain-wall facade inspired by the
lines of all-glass high-rises such as the
UN Building in New York, this skyscraper was Australia's tallest structure
upon completion, and its first International Style building.
[p. 31]

Brazilian Insurance Office Building,
2008
Brasília, Brazil

1958
Antonio Carlos Gomes de Oliveira

[p. 32]

House of Soviets, 2011

Kaliningrad, Russia

1988 (unfinished)
Yulian L. Shvartsbreim

"The Buried Robot" was never completed due to structural problems caused
by building on the top of the ruins
of Königsberg Castle. However, in
2005, to mark Kaliningrad's 60th and
Königsberg's 750th anniversary, and
a visit by President Putin, the exterior
was painted light blue and windows
were installed, a strategy evo-king the
logic of Potemkin villages [p. 33]

Residential Tower, 2007

Saint Petersburg, Russia

1987
V.A. Sokhin, V.M. Sokolov,
P.V. Kurochkin (Lenniiproiekt)

Nicknamed "House on Chicken
Legs", this tower is part of a larger
housing estate, which comprises
four other such towers. The complex
was designed in the mid-1980s, but
the last tower was only completed
in 1993.
[p. 34]

Lisbon Palace of Justice, 2018

Lisbon, Portugal

1970
Januário Gadinho and João Henrique
de Breloes Andresen

The construction of the Lisbon Palace
of Justice lasted for eight years. The
original project included four buildings, forming a square, but only two
were raised. Ironically, or for practical
reasons, the Palace of Justice was built
immediately in front of one of Lisbon's
largest prisons.
[p. 35]

Residential Building, 2019

Kiev, Ukraine

1979
N.G. Brushtinskaya, V.M. Sharapov

As the facade on the street is adorned
with loudspeaker-looking motifs, this
building was designed to have all the
bedrooms open on the inner court-
yard, and all the kitchens on the street,
reducing the inconvenience of the traf-
fic noise coming from it, and making
it thus effectively soundproof.
[p. 36]

Housing Estate, 2007

Vasilyevsky Island, Saint Petersburg,
Russia
1992
architect unknown

The easternmost tip of the Vasilyevsky
Island is framed with a set of twin
housing estates in the shape of trium-
phal arcs. The expanse between the arcs
was unfortunately built up by developers with contemporary condos, ruining
the grand vision of Soviet architects
and their panorama of the Morskaya
embankment seen from the sea.
[p. 37]

Southwestern Bell Building, 2013

Saint Louis, Missouri, USA

1925
Mauran, Russell & Crowell
with I.R. Timlin

At the time of its construction, this
building was the tallest in Missouri
and one of the first in Saint Louis to
use setbacks in the design.
[p. 38]

Manchester Unity Building, 2017

Melbourne, Australia

1932
Marcus Barlow

In spite of the fact that this Art-Deco,
Gothic-inspired office building was
raised in the midst of the Great Depression, its construction lasted only one
year. This record speed was achieved,
among other things, by the imple-
mentation of a construction progress
schedule used to track and manage the
erection of the building, a premiere in
Australia at the time. [p. 39]

Rosomak Sanatorium, 2005

Ustroń-Zawodzie, Poland

1972
Henryk Buszko, Aleksander Franta

Ustroń-Zawodzie is a health resort town designed to host Silesian miners. It contains seventeen pyramid-shaped hotels, and many other structures, all designed by Buszko and Franta. [p. 40]

Cité Administrative, 2014

Lille, France

1965
Serge Menil, Albert Laprade

[p. 41]

Silesian Skyscraper, 2005

Katowice, Poland

1934
S. Bryła, M. Kozłowski

The second-highest Polish building at the time of construction, the Silesian Skyscraper was a symbol of modernity in Silesia, an industrial region in Poland. [p. 42]

Totem Tower, 2016

Paris, France

1979
Michel Andrault, Pierre Parat

One of the original Front-de-Seine towers, its housing units are hung in clusters on a central bearing structure whose orientation optimises the view of the Seine. Florent-Claude Labrouste, Michel Houellebecq's Serotonine's main character, asserts the tower has "several times been classified among the ugliest buildings in Paris." [p. 43]

Stars Housing Estate, 2005

Katowice, Poland

1979
Henryk Buszko, Tadeusz Szewczyk

While the star-shaped floorplan of these towers may look elaborate, it was in fact created to ensure the small flats in these residential towers receive sunlight from two sides. [p. 44]

Grunwald Square Housing Estate, 2006

Wrocław, Poland

1973
Jadwiga Grabowska-Hawrylak

The building is affectionately referred to as "Manhattan", or sometimes "Sedesowce", because of the oval-shaped window niches. "Sedes" is Polish for toilet seat. [p. 45]

"The Corns" Towers, 2006

"1000 Years" Housing Estate, Katowice, Poland
1991
Henryk Buszko, Aleksander Franta

These residential towers on the "1000 Years" housing estate were inspired by Marina City in Chicago, designed by Bertrand Goldberg. [p. 46]

Torres Blancas Housing Estate, 2017

Madrid, Spain

1969
Francisco Javier Sáenz de Oiza

This iconic project, typical of the organicist movement in Spain, brought its designer, Francisco Javier Sáenz de Oiza, recognition at home and abroad. Sáenz de Oiza was one of its first inhabitants and lived there until the end of his life. With the outer wall serving as structural elements, Sáenz de Oiza described the tower as "a tree that starts from the ground". [p. 47]

*Banco De Crédito Del Perú,
Agencia Miraflores*, 2018
Lima, Peru

1979
Jacques Crousse, Jorge Páez

While the building's size, when compared to other skyscrapers, is relatively modest, its monumentality is emphasised by a massive pyramidal base from which vertical elements seem to rise. This bold design is reminiscent of the paper architecture of Futurist Antonio Sant'Elia.
[p. 48]

Strahov Tunnel Ventilation Tower, 2018

Prague, Czech Republic

1980s
Jiří Trnka

There is a kind of spatial incongruity that the ventilation system of the tunnel running under the Strahov Stadium – a horizontal structure – took the form of such a dynamic vertical shape. On the other hand, it is perhaps this formal contradiction that makes the tower so appealing.
[p. 49]

Pardo Office Centre, 2018

Lima, Peru

c. 1969
Miguel Rodrigo Mazuré
[p. 50]

Blok 5 Housing Estate, 2018

Podgorica, Montenegro

1976
Mileta Bojović,
Vukota Tupo Vukotić

With thirteen residential buildings containing 1,800 flats, this estate was designed by Bujović following Vukotić's urban plan but was implemented along the principles of self-management, in which citizens take part in the decisions. Thus, it is set in a sea of greenery with public amenities including schools and health services.
[p. 51]

Bank of Ayudhya, Bang Rak Branch, 2015
Bangkok, Thailand

1970s
Thavisakdi Chandrvirochana

The modern movement in architecture was very prolific in Thailand. One building type in particular developed in original, compelling and intriguing ways: the bank branch. A symbol of modern life, the buildings often displayed futuristically ornamental designs. The Bang Rak Branch is a particularly striking example of this architectural sub-genre. [p. 52]

Izbor Department Store, 2018

Bar, Montenegro

1984
Batrić Mijović

[p. 53]

State Archive, 2012

Warsaw, Poland

1956
Bohdan Pniewski

[p. 54]

House of the Revolution, 2018

Bar, Montenegro

1986
Radmila and Danilo Milošević

This modest round building assumes three functions, differentiated in its three floors: a memorial space, a library with reading room (the Ivo Vučković Library) and the State Archives of Montenegro.
[p. 55]

Salyut Hotel, 2012

Kiev, Ukraine

1984
Avraam Miletsky, N. Slogotskaya,
Vladimir Shevchenko

[p. 56]

Balneological Hospital Water Tower,
2004
Druskininkai, Lithuania

1980
Aušra Šilinskienė,
Romualdas Šilinskas

Located in the spa town of
Druskininkai, the balneological hospital was a place where patients were
treated and cured thanks to the heal-
ing properties of the thermal waters.
A gem of Soviet brutalism and a feat
of concrete engineering, the water
tower was demolished in 2006, when
the hospital was transformed into
a water park. [p. 57]

*Palace of Ceremonial Rites and
Weddings*, 2006
Tbilisi, Georgia

1985
Viktor Dzhorbenadze,
Vazha Orbeladze

As religion was banned from the
official Soviet ideology, the Palaces of
Weddings were, in the Soviet Union,
the venues where civil marriages
were celebrated. A wildly eccentric
building, the suggestive shapes of the
Tbilisi Palace of Ceremonial Rites and
Weddings evoke at the same time the
grandeur of a cathedral, and the
human reproductive organs. [p. 58]

CATA House of Culture, 2014

Cesis, Latvia

1991
Aina Šēnberga

CATA is Latvia's largest and oldest
bus company, founded in 1954, and
state-owned until 1998. The company
was big enough to have its own
house of culture, consisting of a
restaurant, a concert hall, a dancing
hall and many other smaller
multifunctional rooms.
[p. 59]

Auksinés Kopos Vacation Home, 2014

Šventoji, Lithuania

1982
architect unknown

[p. 60]

Balneological Hospital, 2004

Druskininkai, Lithuania

1980
Aušra Šilinskienė, Romualdas Šilinskas

After being shut down at the beginning of 2000, the hospital remained
disused until it was converted into a
waterpark in 2006. This section of the
building is no longer visible.
[p. 61]

VDNKh Main Building, 2006

Tbilisi, Georgia

1961
Levan Mamaladze

VDNKh were permanent exhibition
complexes built in every Soviet capital
to illustrate the innovations and experiences of socialist science, technology,
culture and progressive methods. The
Tbilisi VDNKh opened in 1960 and
Levan Mamaladze supervised the construction of nearly all of the pavilions
over a period of 24 years.
[p. 62]

Dubulti Train Station, 2004

Jūrmala, Latvia

1977
Igors Javeins

[p. 63]

Theme Building, 2012

Los Angeles, California, USA

1961
William Pereira, Charles Luckman

Nowadays an iconic Los Angeles land-mark, the Theme Building is in fact all that remains of a much grander plan for LAX. The first 1959 design had all the terminals connected to a huge glass dome, which would have served as a central hub. While the plan was scaled down, the Theme Building was raised as a reminder and to mark the spot of the original dome. [p. 64]

Angarskyi Pass Trolleybus Stop, 2012

E 105 Highway, Crimea, Russia

1960s
architect unknown

The Angarskyi Pass bus stop marks the highest point (752 metres above sea level) of the longest trolleybus route in the world (81 kilometres), linking Simferopol to Sevastopol, where the road crosses the Crimean Mountains and descends into Alushta.
[p. 65]

Gateway Arch, 2013

Saint Louis, Missouri, USA

1965
Eero Saarinen

Built as a monument to the westward expansion of the United States, the arch was designed by Eero Saarinen in 1947, but was completed only in 1965, after Saarinen's death. With a height of 192 metres, it is the tallest arch in the world. Its summit is reach-able via two flights of stairs, or by trams located in each of the arch's legs.
[p. 66]

Birds of Prey Aviary, 2013

Sofia Zoo, Sofia, Bulgaria

1982
architect unknown

According to an urban legend, the design of this aviary was copied from one in Zurich Zoo. While no such structure exists in Zurich, the zoo aviary in Washington, DC, has a very similar design to that of Sofia. Since all the documentation of the Sofia Zoo has been discarded, the legend prevails.
[p. 67]

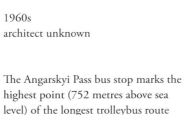

Church of Our Lady of the Scapular, 2013
Pokrzywnica, Poland

1984
Karwoski

The parabola is the main design motif of this small country church. In addition to parabolas being present on the facade, the roof and the side nave, every one of the twelve Stations of the Cross is also paraboloid in shape.
[p. 68]

Church of Santa María Reina, 2018

Lima, Peru

1957
attributed to Guillermo Payet

[p. 69]

Gate, 2015

Iran University of Science and Technology, Tehran, Iran
2004
COVA construction company

The gate's form comes from combin-ing the geometries of two arches: the Iranian ancient arch (inspired by the Tagh-e-Kasra arch) and the Arabic sternum arch. The height of the portal is about twelve metres and is symmetrical on both sides.
[p. 70]

Sanctuary of the Divine Mercy, 2012

Kalisz, Poland

1993
Jerzy Kuźmienko,
Andrzej Fajans

While the design project for this church began in 1958, construction only started in 1977 and was finished sixteen years later. The design owes its shape to the architect's fascination with mathematical constructions and his desire to make the roof out of one huge bended plane.
[p. 71]

Church of Saint Maximilian Kolbe,
2010
Cracow, Poland

1983
Józef Dutkiewicz

The 1980s in Poland saw a boom
in the construction of churches, due
to the liberalisation of construction
regulations, and to the increased
catholic fervour after the election
of John Paul II. It is estimated
that between 1975 and 1989,
2,000 churches were built
in Poland.
[p. 72]

*Church of Our Lady of the Gate of
Dawn,* 2010
Cracow, Poland

1994
Zdzisław Nowakowski (main),
Jan Pociej, Zbigniew Paszkowski

The construction of this church
lasted for more than a decade. Its
roof is inspired by the crown of the
Holy Mary.
[p. 73]

*Church of Saint Maximilian Maria
Kolbe,* 2020
Kolnica, Poland

1986
Andrzej Chwalibóg

[p. 74]

House of Scientists' Creative Work, 2012

Katsiveli, Crimea, Russia

1991
architect unknown

Katsiveli was largely a scientific
village, and contained various institutes with complex equipment, such as
a 22-metre radio telescope, an oceano-
graphic platform or an experimental
storm pool. The institutes gradually
withdrew after 1989, and this sanatorium deteriorated.
[p. 75]

Great Ape House, 2013

Kansas City Zoo, Missouri, USA

1966
Callegari-Kahn construction company

A mid-century Kansas City icon,
this building was disused since 2003,
until it was finally destroyed in 2015,
provoking a wave of nostalgia among
zoo goers. As the local newspaper
Kansas City Star put it when demoli-
tion started: "The space-age Great Ape
House that blasted the Kansas City
Zoo into the future in the 1960s is
falling to Earth." [p. 76]

Racławice Panorama Building, 2017

Wrocław, Poland

1985
Ewa Dziekońska,
Marek Dziekoński

The Racławice Panorama (1893) is a
painting by Jan Styka and Wojciech
Kossak of the Racławice Battle in
1794, when Polish forces defeated the
Russian army. The painting returned
to Poland after WWII, but for over
thirty years the geopolitical situation
delayed the construction of a bespoke
building in which to show it.
[p. 77]

Spanish Cultural Heritage Institute,
2016
Madrid, Spain

1970
Fernando Higueras,
Antonio Miró

From the outside, this arresting
circular building suggests a brutalist
interpretation of the biblical Crown
of Thorns. Inside are studios and labo-
ratories dedicated to the restoration
of priceless works of art, as well as an
impressive library that brings to mind
the limitless, cyclical space of Jorge
Luís Borges's *Library of Babel.*
[p. 78]

*Institute of Robotics and Technical
Cybernetics,* 2007
Saint Petersburg, Russia

1986
S. Savin, B. Artiushin

This building, whose construction
lasted for thirteen years, is an
important symbol of the Soviet
space industry. In 1986, the institute
took part in the design and operation of mobile robots for radiation
reconnaissance and elimination of
the consequences of the Chernobyl
nuclear catastrophe.
[p. 79]

Carillon, 2013

Stone Mountain Park, Atlanta, Georgia, USA
1964
Robert and Company Associates

Originally designed by Welton Beckett, this thirteen-storey redwood-and-steel carillon, known as Carillon Americana, was part of the Coca-Cola Pavilion "The World of Refreshment", at the New York 1964 World's Fair. It is played through an organ located in a small pavilion a couple hundred metres away.
[p. 80]

Open-air Theatre, 2014

Šventoji, Lithuania

1986
Alfredas Gumuliauskas

The theatre has not been used since the early 2000s.
[p. 81]

Memorial House, 2018

Bogetići, Montenegro

1990
Slobodan Vukajlović

Less documented than the *Spomeniks* – monumental abstract sculptures in honour of fallen partisans of the Second World War – the *Spomen Doms* are their architectural equivalent, designed as places of remembrance and as cultural centres.
[p. 82]

Temple of the Community of Christ, 2013

Independence, Missouri, USA

1994
Gyo Obata

The shape of this temple is reminiscent of the spiral shell of the nautilus, culminating with a 91-metre stainless-steel spire.
[p. 83]

Chapel of Thanksgiving, 2013

Dallas, Texas, USA

1976
Phillip Johnson,
John Burgee

[p. 84]

Chamber of Deputies Chapel, 2008

Brasília, Brazil

1960
Oscar Niemeyer

This small structure sits on a terraced roof of the administrative building of the Chamber of Deputies, Brazil's lower house of the National Congress.
[p. 85]

Brighton Municipal Offices, 2017

Melbourne, Australia

1960
Kevin Knight of Oakley and Parkes

The Municipal Building, by and large under the influence of Frank Lloyd Wright's designs – the curved and tapering drum reminding the Guggenheim Museum in New York – is currently used as the Brighton Public Library.
[p. 86]

Orlov Museum of Paleontology, 2018

Moscow, Russia

1987
Y. Platonov, V.M. Kogan, V.P. Nagikh, L.A. Yakovenko

Housing one of the richest paleontological collections in the world, this museum is as striking as it is exuberant and minimalist. From the outside, the building reminds a simplified Teutonic fortress, but once inside, the visitor discovers only four exhibition halls, which are, in turn, huge and meticulously adorned with astonishing bas-relief, sgraffito and metal works. [p. 87]

Monash University Religious Centre,
2017
Melbourne, Australia

1967
Mockridge, Stahle & Mitchell

A small circular building at the very
heart of the university campus, this
temple looks from the outside like the
cooling tower of a miniature nuclear
plant. It was conceived and designed
as a genuinely oecumenical shrine
and consecrated by various religious
congregations: Catholic, Protestant,
Orthodox, Muslim and Jewish.
[p. 88]

Hoover Dam, 2013

Nevada, USA

1936
Gordon Bernie Kaufmann

The world's largest concrete structure
upon completion, the Hoover Dam
was a formidable engineering feat, di-
verting of the Colorado river through
the mountains. Gordon Bernie Kauf-
man, who was brought in to redesign
the exterior, streamlined it and gave
the whole an elegant Art-Deco style.
[p. 89]

Nemunas Hotel Concert Hall, 2003

Druskininkai, Lithuania

1973
Enrikas Tamoševičius, Povilas
Adomaitis

The original building, considered of
"no architectural, cultural nor aesthetic value", was destroyed
in 2009 and replaced by a
contemporary structure.
[p. 90]

Dining Hall, 2012

Donbass Sanatorium, Massandra,
Crimea, Russia
1964
Anatoly Polyansky,
V.A. Somov

[p. 91]

*Jimmy Carter Presidential Library and
Museum,* 2013
Atlanta, Georgia, USA

1986
Jova, Daniels, Busby of Atlanta and
Lawton, Umemura & Yamamoto
of Honolulu
[p. 92]

Museum of Archaeology, 2006

Tbilisi, Georgia

1988
Shota Kavlashvili,
Shota Gvantseladze

A gem of late Soviet modernism, this
building is composed of a set of three
intertwined round structures, half
sunken in what appears to be a deserted steppe, but is in fact, in one of
the suburbs of Tbilisi. Housing a collection accounting for the continuous
human settlement in the Tbilisi area
for 6,000 years, the building has been
disused for the last ten years. [p. 93]

Church of Saint Jan Kanty, 2010

Cracow, Poland

1992
Krzysztof Bień

The construction of this church,
affectionately nicknamed U-Boot,
lasted for nearly a decade.
[p. 94]

VDNKh Pavilion no. 10, 2006

Tbilisi, Georgia

1984
Levan Mamaladze

[p. 95]

Dining Hall, 2015

Kibbutz Sha'ar HaGolan, Israel

1967
Samuel Mestechkin

[p. 96]

Fishing Terminal Canopy, 2018

Pucusana, Peru

c. 1960
architect unknown

An elegant structure designed to shelter fishermen when they unload their catch, it might have been inspired by Josep Lluís Sert's design for the church in Puerto Ordaz, Venezuela, which made the cover of *Arquitecto Peruano* in September 1953.
[p. 97]

Bathing Pool, 2011

Kaliningrad, Russia

1982
Nikolai Nikolaevich Batakov, Pavel Mikhailovich Gorbach

The bathing pool is one of the attractions of the Kaliningrad Zoo's Children's Town, which remains in operation.
[p. 98]

Customs and Firefighting Quarter, 2010

International Fairgrounds, Tripoli, Lebanon
1975 (unfinished)
Oscar Niemeyer

[p. 99]

Civic Offices Council Chamber, 2017

Altona, Australia

1963
Robert Warren

This local landmark illustrates the progressive and forward-thinking philosophy of the City of Altona, and its rapid development from its inception in 1957 to the construction of the new municipal complex in 1963. The distinctive domed form was inspired by buildings of the time such as Romberg and Boyd's Academy of Science building in Canberra. [p. 100]

Shine Dome, 2017

Canberra, Australia

1958
Roy Grounds

Home to the Australian Academy of Science, the Shine Dome is one of Australia's iconic modernist landmarks. Its minimalist yet futuristic design was imagined to reflect the innovative nature of science. It is one of those rare buildings in which form and content are perfectly symbiotic, and this is mirrored beautifully in its enlightening name. [p. 101]

Sēnīte Restaurant, 2014

A2 Highway, near Krustiņi, Latvia

1967
Linards Skuja, Andris Bite, Rūdolfam Ozoliņam

An engineering masterpiece at the time and the first concrete shell construction of its kind in Latvia, the Sēnīte (mushroom) restaurant has been abandoned since the early 2000s.
[p. 102]

Pol'ana Hotel, 2015

Tatranská Javorina, Slovakia

1977
Štefan Ďurkovič, Julián Hauskrecht, František Husovský, Štefan Svetko

This hotel, which was disused since the early 2000s until recently, is currently working under the name Hotel Monfort. It was originally a recreational facility of the Central Committee of the Communist Party of Czechoslovakia in Javorina.
[p. 103]

Concert Shell, 2010

International Fairgrounds, Tripoli, Lebanon
1975 (unfinished)
Oscar Niemeyer

[p. 104]

Gas Station, 2018

Marrakech, Morocco

1958
Jean-François Zevaco

Change, movement and speed are all illustrations of the idea of progress which lay at the core of the modernist ethos. It is therefore not surprising that petrol stations should adopt curved and aero-dynamic shapes, such as this petrol station in Marrakech. Designed by prominent modernist architect, Jean-François Zevaco.
[p. 105]

Bus Stop, 2004

Lithuania

1970s
architect unknown

[p. 106]

Bus Stop, 2012

Foros, Crimea, Russia

1970s
architect unknown

[p. 107]

Bus Stop, 2012

Partenit, Crimea, Russia

1970s
architect unknown

[p. 108]

Bus Stop, 2003

Lithuania

1970s
architect unknown

[p. 109]

Dead Sea Museum and Visitor Center, 2015
Neve Zohar, Israel

1971
Samuel Mestechkin

This complex, which also comprises youth hostel, has been disused since the mid-1990s. Very carefully designed, the windows of the museum, whose trapezoidal shape reflects that of the building, were adorned with a bean shaped cut-out form made out of steel, which represents the Dead Sea itself, at the time when it was one large basin, and not two small pools. [p. 110]

Bus Station, 2004

Kupiškis, Lithuania

1970s
architect unknown

While the design of bus stops in Soviet Lithuania often displayed bold and organic forms, this bus station in Kupiškis was, on the contrary, sleek and minimalist. It was destroyed in the mid-2010s to be replaced by an anonymous contemporary structure.
[p. 111]

First Federal Savings and Loan Association Branch, 2012
Texarkana, Texas/Arkansas, USA

1976
Ann Bintliff of Bintliff, Bell and Holderness Architects

Located on the Arkansas side of Texarkana, the building has been vacant since 2011.
[p. 112]

Palace of Pioneers, 2018

Moscow, Russia

1962
F. Novikov, V. Egerev, V. Kubasov, B. Palui, I. Pokrovsky, M. Khazhakyan

Young Pioneers were, in the USSR, an institution akin to the Scout Movement, but state sponsored and ideologically oriented. This was one of the first public buildings departing from the socialist-realist aesthetics. It was the centrepiece of the Young Pioneer's complex, housing an observatory, a theatre, a stadium and parading grounds. [p. 113]

Church of Jesus Christ of Latter-day Saints Visitors' Center, 2013
Independence, Missouri, USA

1971
Emil Fetzer

The visitors' centre was designed by Emil Fetzer, who held the position of chief architect at the Mormon Church between 1965 and 1986.
[p. 114]

Lebanese Pavilion, 2010

International Fairgrounds, Tripoli, Lebanon
1975 (unfinished)
Oscar Niemeyer

[p. 115]

Palace of Justice, 2008

Brasília, Brazil

1957
Oscar Niemeyer

[p. 116]

Tharmaratnam Residence, 2013

Colombo, Sri Lanka

1970
Valentine Gunasekara

[p. 117]

Cross-City Line Powiśle Station Upper Entrance, 2004
Warsaw, Poland

1963
Arseniusz Romanowicz, Piotr Szymaniak

With yet another paraboloid shape for this station of the Warsaw suburban train line, the roof of this building, which is parallel to the stairs, goes down to the train platforms.
[p. 118]

Cross-City Line Ochota Station, 2012

Warsaw Poland

1963
Arseniusz Romanowicz, Piotr Szymaniak

The design of the hyperbolic paraboloid roof is based on a square, where two diagonal vertices are raised up, while the two others are held down, supporting the roof only on these two points. It is supposed to imitate the way the tense fabric of tents reacts when twisted.
[p. 119]

Pride Cleaners, 2012

Chicago, Illinois, USA

1959
Gerald Siegwart

This building is considered one of the best examples of Googie architecture in Chicago, and continues to this day to fulfil its original function. [p. 120]

Roy's Motel and Café, 2012

Amboy, California, USA

1959
Herman "Buster" Burris

Located on Route 66, Amboy became a ghost town in the 1970s following the opening of the Interstate I-72. Roy's café started as a gas station in 1939, and in the late 1940s expanded into a café and motel. Buster Burris, founder Roy Crowl's son-in-law, erected the motel single-handedly on the basis of modern blueprints bought from an LA architectural firm. [p. 121]

Church of Our Lady of Fatima, 2008

Brasília, Brazil

1958
Oscar Niemeyer

[p. 122]

Church of Jesus the Good Shepherd, 2010

Cracow, Poland

1974
Wojciech Maria Pietrzyk

[p. 123]

Church of the Exaltation of the Holy Cross, 2007

Żory-Rój, Poland

1959
Tadeusz Augustynek

[p. 124]

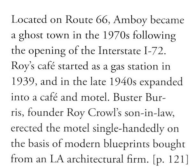

Church of Holy Hedwig, 2007

Pszczyna, Poland

1989
Antoni Czernow

[p. 125]

All Saints Anglican Church, 2017

Rosebud, Australia

1963
Wystan Widdows,
David Caldwell

[p. 126]

House of Culture, 2014

Kibbutz HaOgen, Israel

1966
Menachem Beer

Two types of buildings are central in the organisation of every kibbutz: the dining hall and the house of culture. For the last decade, however, the privatisation of kibbutzim has led to the closing of many houses of culture, such as in Kibbutz HaOgen which has been disused since the early 2010s. It is adorned with a monumental mosaic by Shraga Weil. [p. 127]

Memorial House, 2017

Tjentište, Bosnia and Herzegovina

1974
Ranko Radović

This is part of a larger complex commemorating the Battle of Sutjeska in 1943, one of the bloodiest episodes of the Second World War in Yugoslavia. The complex also contained a museum, which was looted after 1991, but the concrete, bunker-like Memorial House still stands and was put on the UNESCO World Heritage List in 2012. [p. 128]

Church of the Lord Jesus the Good Shepherd, 2017

Rudy-Rysie, Poland

1973
Tadeusz Gawłowsk

[p. 129]

Strumok Roadside Restaurant, 2019

Kiev, Ukraine

1970s
architect unknown

[p. 130]

House of Culture, 2014

Saulkrasti, Latvia

1980
Viktors Zilgalvis

The Saulkrasti House of Culture has been disused since the early 2000s. In the 1980s it housed a quite popular discotheque called "Parole", frequented even by the golden youth from Riga.
[p. 131]

Motel Miljevina, 2017

Miljevina, Bosnia and Herzegovina

1973
architect unknown

Once a high-end holiday resort, the hotel became deserted with the break-up of Yugoslavia. It remains notoriously remembered in the region for being the place where war crimes were perpetrated.
[p. 132]

Church of the Body of Christ, 2007

Wrzosowa, Poland

1978
Stanisław Kwaśniewicz

[p. 133]

House of Ritual Services, 2010

Vilnius, Lithuania

1987
Česlovas Mazūras

In the Soviet Union, as religion was banned from official ideology, houses of ritual services were built to serve as secular mourning edifices. The Vilnius House of Ritual Services, whose construction lasted twelve years, consists of two buildings that house twelve grieving rooms.
[p. 134]

Sutjeska Memorial Monument, 2017

Tjentište, Bosnia and Herzegovina

1971
Miodrag Živković,
Đorđe Zloković

This monument perpetuates the memory of the Battle of Sutjeska, one of the grimmer episodes of World War II in Yugoslavia. It is one of Yugoslavia's most famous Spomeniks. The Sutjeska monument is not only a sculptural masterpiece, it is also a tour de force of spatial design, the concrete shapes masterly towering the valley below.
[p. 135]

Tancredo Neves Pantheon of Fatherland and Freedom, 2008

Brasília, Brazil

1986
Oscar Niemeyer

The dove-shaped cenotaph was built following the death of Tancredo Neves, Brazil's first elected civilian president since the military coup twenty years earlier. It is dedicated to this national hero, but unlike other pantheons it is not a mausoleum and does not contain any tomb.
[p. 136]

Crematorium, 2012

Kiev, Ukraine

1975
Avraam Miletsky

[p. 137]

House of Culture for Youth, 2014

Kibbutz Heftziba, Israel

1968
Ziva Armoni

This house of culture, designed by one of the few women architects working in Israel after the Second World War, was considered groundbreaking at the time of completion, with its multi-functional partitioned plan, opening on the surrounding landscape. It has been disused since the early 2010s.
[p. 138]

Palace of Weddings, 2010

Vilnius, Lithuania

1974
Gediminas Baravykas

The Vilnius Palace of Weddings was the first building in Lithuania built exclusively for the purpose of marriage ceremonies.
[p. 139]

Movie Theatre, 2014

Valgeranna, Estonia

1979
Meeli Truu, Raine Karp

The disused movie theatre is part of a sports and recreational complex originally built for the Council of Ministers of the Estonian SSR.
[p. 140]

Daugavkrasti Hotel, 2014

Jēkabpils, Latvia

1982
Vanda Baulina

Originally built as a local forestry department, this building is now protected on a list of cultural monuments of state importance.
[p. 141]

Renaissance Cinema, 2012

Daugavpils, Latvia

1978
Olerts Krauklis,
Maija Rita Skalberga

[p. 142]

Archive Building, 2012

Atlanta, Georgia, USA

1965
A. Thomas Bradbury

This building was often described as The White Ice Cube due to its shape and semitransparent marble elevations. In 1998, engineers determined that the building was sinking and the Georgia Archives were relocated to a new home in 2003. The building was destroyed in 2017 through a controlled implosion.
[p. 143]

Bank of Manhattan Trust Company,
2008
New York, NY, USA

1929
architect unknown

It is interesting to see how the simplified shape and ornamentation of this neo-Romanesque building resulted in a proto-minimalist structure, modest yet imposing in its expression. The building changed ownership (but also function) many times over the years – from a bank, it became a health centre before being turned back into a bank again. [p. 144]

House of Culture, 2012

Alupka, Crimea, Russia

1977
architect unknown

The House of Culture was, in every village of the USSR, place dedicated to cultural activities. After 1991, many houses of culture closed down for financial reasons. This building, disused since 2012, reopened its doors in 2020 after renovations, which unfortunately ruined the original facade.
[p. 145]

Nuclear Power Plant, 2004

Ignalina, Lithuania

1984
architect unknown

This nuclear power plant, sharing a similar design to Chernobyl, started working in 1984. The construction of the third reactor was halted because of the Chernobyl catastrophe, and the plant was finally shut down in 2009 due to European Union ecology and security restrictions.
[p. 146]

Universal Store, 2012

Uhlove, Crimea, Russia

1980s
architect unknown

This store was built according to a standard project of the TsentroSoyuzProiekt Design Institute, and modified by local architects.
[p. 147]

Silesian Institute of Science, 2014

Katowice, Poland

1977
Stanisław Kwaśniewicz

The building's design is based on a set of interconnected squares. The low and compact mass of the building was given lightness by shearing the facade, and placing the structure on pilotis. The Silesian Institute of Science was closed down in 1992 and the building has been disused ever since.
[p. 148]

Hilda Melvin and Gerard Furst Library,
2015
Mitzpe Ramon, Israel

1960s
David Best, Adam Eyal

[p. 149]

VDNKh Pavilion no. 7, 2006

Tbilisi, Georgia

1971
D. Paninashvili, L. Mamaladze,
V. Nasaridze, V. Peykrishvili

The Tbilisi VDNKh (The Exhibitions of the Achievements of the National Economy of the USSR) opened in 1961. Pavilion no. 7, constructed a decade later, is adorned with *Creativity*, a sculpture by Levan Mamaladze, the chief architect of the whole complex.
[p. 150]

Russian Academy of Sciences, 2018

Moscow, Russia

1988
Yuri Platonov

This is one of the most extravagant and baroque pieces of Soviet modernism. Adorned with exuberant bronze sculptures, pink granite cladding and copper-tinted windows, its twin towers are crowned with an intricate gilded structure seemingly taken straight out of Fritz Lang's *Metropolis*. Not surprisingly, the locals have nicknamed the complex "The Brain". [p. 151]

Pavilion at the Nymphengarten, 2016

Karlsruhe, Germany

1964
State Building Administration of
Baden-Württemberg

This elegant, yet anonymously signed
glass-and-steel International style
structure was built to house the
collections of the state library whose
building had been ravaged during the
Second World War. It retained this
function for only a dozen years, before
being used as an annex to the Museum
of Natural History. [p. 152]

Bus Station, 2011

Kaliningrad, Russia

1971
A.I. Garanina, M.T. Suslov

This bus station was built according to
standardised plans from the Leningrad
branch of the Giproavtotrans Design
Institute. Modifications by local
architects include a new facade and
clock tower.
[p. 153]

Sports Palace, 2012

Frunze Kolkhoz, Crimea, Russia

1987
architect unknown

This sports palace, which was built by
the residents of the Frunze Kolkhoz,
was drawn from a standard architectural design of the Mezentsev TsNIIEP
design institute.
[p. 154]

Latter Day Saints Auditorium, 2013

Independence, Missouri, USA

1958
architect unknown

Groundbreaking construction began
in 1926 and the building was only
completed in 1958. The Conference
Chamber was originally supposed
to be about 66 per cent larger than
it is today according to the vision of
Frederick M. Smith. Construction
was virtually halted during the Great
Depression when the church struggled
under massive debt. [p. 155]

Centennial Hall, 2017

Wrocław, Poland

1913
Max Berg,
Günther Trauer

Built to mark the 100th anniversary
of Prussia's 1813 War of Liberation
against Napoleon, this is a landmark
of reinforced concrete architecture it
later became a key reference for this
type of architecture. I always found
it a beautiful coincidence that the
architect's name, Berg, would so won-
derfully resonate with a building that
looks like a mountain. [p. 156]

Urania Sports Hall, 2005

Olsztyn, Poland

1978
Wiesław Piątkowski,
Henryk Gotz

The Urania Sports Hall in Olsztyn
is a copy the Okrąglak Sports Hall
in Opole. The first secretary of the
Communist Party in Olsztyn had
previously held the same function in
Opole, and re-used the design of the
Okrąglak (Round One) in Olsztyn.
[p. 157]

*Institute of Scientific and Technical
Information*, 2012
Kiev, Ukraine

1971
Florian Yuryev,
L. Novikov

Architect Florian Yuryev conceived a
new form of art: a synthesis of music,
light and colour, for which he designed a special egg-shaped hall. Construction was difficult, and completed
only thanks to the protection of the
KGB. However, instead of a colour-
light theatre, it became the cinema of
the Institute of Scientific Information.
Today it is largely disused. [p. 158]

Spodek Sports Hall, 2014

Katowice, Poland

1971
Maciej Gintowt, Maciej Krasiński,
Jerzy Hryniewiecki

This was one of the first major
structures to employ the principle
of tensegrity – a term coined by
Buckminster Fuller that combines
tension and integrity – to create
stability between stretched and
pressed elements.
[p. 159]

Abandoned Solar Radio Telescope, 2012

Crimean Laser Observatory, Katsiveli, Crimea, Russia
mid-1940s
architect unknown

This radio telescope is part of the larger astrophysical complex in Katsiveli. This particular structure was probably never finished and has been abandoned since the early 1950s. [p. 160]

Concert Shell, 2002

Gdynia, Poland

1962
Błaszkowiak

[p. 161]

National Museum of the Republic, 2008

Brasília, Brazil

2006
Oscar Niemeyer

Set on Brasília's monumental axis, the National Museum of the Republic is part of the Cultural Complex of the Republic, which comprises the Brazilian National Library, also designed by Oscar Niemeyer. [p. 162]

Experimental Theatre, 2010

International Fairgrounds, Tripoli, Lebanon
1975 (unfinished)
Oscar Niemeyer

During, the Lebanese Civil War, the Tripoli International Fairgrounds were used as a post for the occupying Syrian army. In 2004, the Tripoli Chamber of Commerce announced its plan to convert it into a Disneyland-type theme park. Subsequently, in 2006, the fairgrounds were added to the World Monuments Fund Watch List of 100 Most Endangered Sites. [p. 163]

Arena Multi-purpose Hall, 2005

Poznan, Poland

1974
Jerzy Turzeniecki

The Arena is an almost 1:1 copy of the Palazzetto dello Sport in Rome, designed by Annibale Vitellozzi and Pier Luigi Nervi in the 1950s. [p. 164]

Legia Stadium Ticket Booth, 2004

Warsaw, Poland

1968
Tadeusz Rupiński

This structure was destroyed in 2008. [p. 165]

Rannapere Retirement Home, 2014

Haabneeme, Estonia

1974
Rein Veber

The Rannapere Retirement Home was designed for the members of the Kirov Model Fishing Farm. The upper floor was added after 2000 and remains unfinished. [p. 166]

Poster Museum, 2011

Warsaw, Poland

1974
Jacek K. Cydzik i Barbara Kossuth

The New Gallery, located behind the baroque Wilanów Palace, houses the Poster Museum and was created by transforming a former riding hall built in 1845–55 and designed by Franciszek Maria Lanci. [p. 167]

Watsungwej Printing School, 2015

Bangkok, Thailand

1970s
architect unknown

The Watsungwej printing school, founded in 1932 and originally located in another, smaller building across the street, is the oldest technical school of that type in Thailand. [p. 168]

Guildhall West Wing, 2017

London, UK

1974
Giles Gilbert Scott and Richard Gilbert Scott

Giles Scott was commissioned to build an extension to the Guildhall in the 1950s. After his death in 1960, it was ultimately finished by his son, Richard Scott. The West Wing's eccentric design, an example of what Ernő Goldfinger dismissed as "pop modern", beautifully contrasts with the austerity of the medieval gothic Guildhall, set in front of it. [p. 169]

VDNKh Pavilion no. 9 "Intra-Trade", 2011

Kiev, Ukraine

1964
architect unknown

The Kiev VDNKh opened in 1959 and Pavilion no. 9 – whose design was originally used in the Czechoslovakian agricultural exhibition – was built in 1964. [p. 170]

Municipal House of Sports, 2010

Tarnów, Poland

1972
Bogumił Zaufal, Stanisław Karpiel, Władysław Cukier, Zbigniew S. Bielak

A glass-encased cafeteria, which serves nowadays as a gym, divides the interior of the building in two halves, with a basketball field in one part and a swimming pool in the other. [p. 171]

Eames House, 2012

Pacific Palisades, California, USA

1949
Ray and Charles Eames

The Eames House was built from prefabricated materials ordered from catalogues. Also known as Case Study House #8, it was part of a programme, spearheaded by *Arts & Architecture* publisher John Entenza, where architects were encouraged to employ materials and techniques derived from the experiences of the Second World War. [p. 172]

Yellow Housing Estate, 2005

Warsaw, Poland

1986
Metalleichtbaukombinat Leipzig

The Lipsk and Berlin type buildings were popular systems of prefabricated elements imported to Poland from East Germany in the 1970s. The buildings, featuring aluminium frames filled with tempered stained glass in vibrant colours, have been demolished due to dangerous asbestos content. This particular building was destroyed in 2013. [p. 173]

Banque Lombard Odier & Cie, 2017

Geneva, Switzerland

1970s
architect unknown

With its golden facade, adorned with protruding diamond-shaped ornaments, this building used to belong to one of Switzerland's oldest private banks. The light installation on its roof, showcasing the word "dimanche" ("Sunday" in French), a humorous injunction to rest, is the work of artist Christian-Robert Tissot. [p. 174]

Rector's Office, 2017
Nicolaus Copernicus University Campus, Toruń, Poland

1972
Marek Różański

This campus – whose rectorate is an integral part – is considered one of the most important achievements of late modernism in Poland. Minimalist and rational, its architecture and urban design followed the functional division of buildings according to their purpose: science and education; social and cultural life; and administrative. [p. 175]

Housing Super-Unit, 2006

Katowice, Poland

1972
Mieczysław Król

Inspired by Le Corbusier's Housing Unit, it bore until 1994 on its roof the slogan "Our Thoughts, Hearts and Deeds we dedicate to you, Socialist Homeland."
[p. 176]

Superquadra South 104, 2008

Brasília, Brazil

1960
Lucio Costa

Superquadras were conceived as autonomous housing districts in Brasília, with their own school, playgrounds and commercial areas. Typically, it is a six-storey building placed on pilotis, but the design of particular superquadras varies.
[p. 177]

Hanoi Children's Palace, 2019

Hanoi, Vietnam

1976
Le Van Lan

Children's Palaces were, in socialist countries, public recreation centres where children engage in extracurricular activities. The Hanoi Children's Palace, considered today a modernist masterpiece, was built at the end of the Vietnam War – and thus at a time of economic hardship – and was the expression of the government's engagement in the future of the nation.
[p. 178]

Parking Lot, 2013

Texarkana, Texas/Arkansas, USA

date unknown
architect unknown

This garage, located on the Texas side of Texarkana, was used by the employees of the First Federal Savings and Loan Association branch located on the other side of State Line Avenue (i.e. in Arkansas).
[p. 179]

House of Sports and Culture, 2014

Former Linda Kolkhoz,
Võru, Estonia
1973
Toomas Rein

[p. 180]

National Historical Museum, 2013

Sofia, Bulgaria

1973
Alexander Georgiev Barov

Opened in 1973, the Boyana Residence commemorated the thirtieth anniversary of the 1944 coup d'état and "The Victory of Socialist Revolution in Bulgaria". It was a lavish and luxurious complex used by the highest dignitaries of the state until the fall of communism in Bulgaria and was turned into the National Historical Museum in 2000. [p. 181]

Rowing Club, 2005

Warsaw, Poland

1948
Arseniusz Romanowicz,
Piotr Szymaniak

Originally designed as a YMCA facility, this rowing club was built thanks to an American financial backer as part of the post-war reconstruction of Warsaw after the Second World War.
[p. 182]

VDNKh Pavilion no. 19 "Common Consumption Goods", 2012
Kiev, Ukraine

1971
Boris Zhezherin

[p. 183]

Klimatopavilon, 2005

Ministry of Internal Affairs Sanatorium, Yevpatoriya, Crimea, Russia
1970s
architect unknown

The Klimatopavilon is the part of the sanatorium where one is supposed to rest in cabins located directly above the sea, in order to restore one's health, thanks to the curative properties of marine air. It is based on a design by Anatoly Polyansky.
[p. 184]

Sunbathing Platform, 2012

Central Military Clinical Sanatorium, Alupka, Crimea, Russia
date unknown
architect unkown

In 2010, the Central Military Clinical Sanatorium in Alupka was recognised as "one of the top 10 most dangerous sanatoria in Crimea" by the Ukrainian Ministry of Health due to the extremely poor condition of its buildings.
[p. 185]

Onogošt Hotel Garden Pavilion, 2018

Nikšić, Montenegro

1982
Ivan and Tihomir Štraus

[p. 186]

Ministry of Highways, 2006

Tbilisi, Georgia

1974
George Chakhava, Zurab Jalaghania, Temur Tkhilava, V. Kimberg

The eighteen-storey construction is based on the concept of Space City, whose idea is to give space below the building back to natu-re. Its structure also references the iconic Volkenbugel (Iron-Cloud), an unbuilt project for horizontal sky-scrapers imagined by El Lissitzky in the early 1920s. The building was acquired by the Bank of Georgia in 2007. [p. 187]

279

Palace of Culture and Sports of the Ministry of the Interior, 2010
Vilnius, Lithuania

1982
Algimantas Mačiulis

Whereas this buiding was designed as a late modernist and quite typical Soviet-style House of Culture, its fate ultimately turned against the USSR, as played its part in what would become the Lithuanian Independence movement – namely, by hosting the rock festival Lithuanika.
[p. 188]

House of Culture, 2015

Kibbutz Kfar Blum, Israel

1983
M. Shilon

[p. 189]

Slovak National Archives, 2015

Bratislava, Slovakia

1983
Vladimir Dedeček

Evoking filing cabinets aligned next to each other, from one side, and drawers halfway opened, from the other, this building is considered to be one of Dedeček's greatest achievements. It used to sit, all by itself, on top of a hill, but its vicinity is now flooded by massive real-estate investments.
[p. 190]

Palace of Ritual Services, 2014

Pärnu, Estonia

1976
Anne Siht

[p. 191]

House of Culture, 2014

Former Marytės Melninkaitės
Kolkhoz, Dotnuva, Lithuania
1980
B. Barzdžiūnas, V. Budrys

This building has been empty since
the early 2000s.
[p. 192]

House of Culture, 2014

Former "Tamsalu" Kolkhoz, Tamsalu,
Estonia
1981
Maara Metsal

The building is currently being used as
a warehouse for agricultural machinery.
[p. 193]

Dining Hall, 2014

Kibbutz Mishmar HaNegev, Israel

1976
Yoska Rusiansky

[p. 194]

Tarnovia Hotel, 2012

Tarnów, Poland

1975
A. Kowalewski

The mosaic represents the 1850 siege
of Aleppo, where Tarnów-born general
Joseph Bem played an important role,
and eventually died, after converting
to Islam.
[p. 195]

Trade Union Cultural Centre, 2006

Tbilisi, Georgia

1970s
G. Metonidze

The mural on the facade was designed
by the famous and controversial artist
Zurab Tsereteli, renowned for making
monumental sculptures, and who
has been President of the Russian
Academy of Arts since 1997.
[p. 196]

Shams Building, 2010

Beirut, Lebanon

1957
Joseph Philippe Karam

[p. 197]

Slovak National Gallery, 2015

Bratislava, Slovakia

1977
Vladimir Dedeček

This controversial building was
designed as a huge bridge sitting
on top of a seventeenth-century
baroque palace. Its construction
spanned a decade.
[p. 198]

Równica Sanatorium, 2006

Ustroń-Zawodzie, Poland

1970
Henryk Buszko, Aleksander Franta,
Tadeusz Szewczyk

The sanatorium was designed in
accordance to Le Corbusier's "Five
Points of Modern Architecture" and is
considered to be the most important
building in this the spa town.
[p. 199]

Pelegrin Hotel, 2018

Kupari, Croatia

1963
David Finci

This hotel was part of a larger touristic complex originally founded in the 1920s by the Czech Spa Entreprise. Heavily developed during the Yugoslav period, the complex comprised, at its height, as many as six hotels and a camping site – even Marshall Tito had a villa nearby. It was badly damaged during the Yugoslav War and has remained disused since then. [p. 200]

Colonial Mutual Building, 2017

Canberra, Australia

1968
Towell, Rippon and Associates

A distinctive Canberra mid-century landmark, this building was bought recently by developers and is at risk of being demolished.
[p. 201]

House of Composers' Creative Work, 2006

Borjomi, Georgia

1982
Sh. Davitashvili, N. Solovyeva, M. Zhuruli, G. Metonidze, N. Karichashvili
[p. 202]

College of Liberal Arts and Sciences Building, 2011

University of Illinois Campus, Chicago, Illinois, USA
1968
Walter Netsch

[p. 203]

Uni Dufour Building, 2017

Geneva, Switzerland

1974
Werner Francesco, Gilbert Paux and Jacques Vicari

Inspired by Le Corbusier's modular designs, this building is part of the University of Geneva. Following a competition organised in 1995 to animate the building, time counters are installed on the cells of the facade.
[p. 204]

Church of Saint Michael, 2016

Karlsruhe, Germany

1965
Werner Groh

Based on a square, and conforming to the recommendations enshrined in the Second Vatican Council (1962–5), the design of this church brings the faithful closer to the priest celebrating Mass.
[p. 205]

Municipality Council Building, 2018

Essaouira, Morocco

1980s
architect unknown

[p. 206]

Town Hall, 2018

Agadir, Morocco

1960
Emile Duhon

Agadir was ravaged in 1960 by the most destructive earthquake in Moroccan history. The city was rebuilt from scratch according to modernist principles. The Town Hall is a prominent achievement of that period: a simple box adorned with complex geometric motifs, reminiscent of the designs of traditional Muslim architecture. [p. 207]

Nightingale Olympic Co. Building,
2015
Bangkok, Thailand

1966
architect unknown

This is Bangkok's oldest department store, founded in 1930. The current building was raised later. It still belongs to the same owners, a family of merchants who have kept the interior untouched since the 1960s. evoking its raison d'être as a consumers' paradise, its slogan reads: "Hub of Sporting Goods, King of Musical Instruments, Queen of Cosmetics." [p. 208]

Residential Building, 2015

Tehran, Iran

1970s
architect unknown

The only information about this unostentatious yet muscular-looking structure was that it used to house a shop selling topographic and geodetic tools. I find quite ironic – and amusing – that the most mysterious building in this *Atlas* would actually sell tools to make atlases.
[p. 209]

Residential Building, 2015

Bangkok, Thailand

1970s
architect unknown

[p. 210]

Hotel Biserna Obala, 2008

Čanj, Montenegro

1983
Radmila and Danilo Milošević

[p. 211]

Hotel Medea, 2006

Batumi, Georgia

1987
Alexander Bakradze

This former luxury hotel on the Black Sea had been inhabited for a decade by Abkhaz refugees before being destroyed in 2006, to be replaced by a Radisson Blu chain hotel.
[p. 212]

Residential Building, 2018

Lima, Peru

c. 1968
architect unknown

Started in 1968, construction halted in the 1980s when the developer ran out of funds. Still, those owners who had bought their flats settled in, despite the building's incomplete state. An engineering study revealed that in an earthquake the building could collapse due to the thinness of its columns and the time the raw concrete was exposed to moisture. [p. 213]

Hotel Meskheti, 2006

Batumi, Georgia

early 1980s
Koridze

This hotel also became a shelter for Abkhaz refugees and was destroyed in 2007.
[p. 214]

Chorhoz Sanatorium, 2006

Kobuleti, Georgia

date unknown
architect unknown

The original Chorhoz Sanatorium was a socialist-realist edifice built in the early 1950s. Plans to modernise it, and add another modernist wing to it, were undertaken, but put to a halt by the collapse of the Soviet Union, and the concrete structure remains unfinished. The sanatorium has been disused ever since.
[p. 215]

Dilapidated Hotel, 2006

Borjomi, Georgia

1980s
architect unknown

This building has since been refurbished and is currently used as a guest house.
[p. 216]

Guboja Hotel and Sanatorium, 2014

Šventoji, Lithuania

1976
Rimantas Buivydas

Once an exclusive sanatorium, built for the civil servants of the ministry of meat and dairy products, this building has been disused since 1993.
[p. 217]

Museum for Contemporary Art, 2015

Tehran, Iran

1977
Kamran Diba

Commissioned by the former Queen of Iran, Farah Pahlavi, and designed by her cousin, this museum stores the largest collection of Western modern art outside of Europe and North America.
[p. 218]

New Students House, 2018

Podgorica, Montenegro

1978
Milan Popović

[p. 219]

El Fath Housing Estate, 2018

Essaouira, Morocco

1960s
architect unknown

Designed in the 1960s, but only inhabited since 1972, this social housing estate, commissioned by the Caisse de Dépôt et de Gestion, suffers from many structural problems linked to the fact that it was built on a flood zone.
[p. 220]

Ramot Polin Housing Estate, 2014

Jerusalem, Israel

1975
Zvi Hecker

The 720-unit complex was part of an attempt to create large-scale iconic architecture in the territories conquered during the Six Day War.
[p. 221]

Lino Swimming Pool, 2014

Palanga, Lithuania

1984
Algimantas Lėckas, Saulius Šarkinas, L. Merkinas

This building and the Rugelis Holiday Complex (see pp. 222 and 242) are two of the many structu-res built in Vanagupé, the satellite city of Palanga. Built from scratch, Vanagupé was planned as a city for 16,000 holiday-goers. Built along a green axis with the pool at its centre, Vanagupé is one of the last examples of recreational Soviet urbanism on such a scale. [p. 222]

Private Villa, 2006

Warsaw, Poland

1970s
architect unknown

[p. 223]

House of Composers' Union, 2010

Vilnius, Lithuania

1966
Vytautas Čekanauskas

With an emphasis on the use of natural materials, the House of Composer's Union was Influenced by Finnish architecture. The structure comprises several club rooms and a concert hall.
[p. 224]

Technical School Auditorium, 2014

Former "Jäneda" Sovkhoz, Jäneda, Estonia
1975
Valve Pormeister

[p. 225]

Bowling Pavilion, 2014

Šventoji, Lithuania

date unknown
architect unknown

This wooden structure is part of a larger holiday complex, the Golden Dunes hotel, and was one of the rare places where holiday-goers could bowl in the former Soviet Lithuania. It is currently disused.
[p. 226]

Mladost Hotel, 2017

Tjentište, Bosnia and Herzegovina

1963
Jug Milić

[p. 227]

Kormoran Resort, 2006

Olsztyn, Poland

1974
A. Kowalewski

This luxury estate was built for the First Secretary of the Polish Communist Party, Edward Gierek. Through the years, numerous eminent figures of Polish politics were hosted there as the apartment remained property of the state. The original structure was demolished and a new hotel was built on the same foundations.
[p. 228]

Pyramid, 2010

International Fairgrounds, Tripoli, Lebanon
1975 (unfinished)
Oscar Niemeyer

[p. 229]

Church of the Immaculate Heart of Our Lady Mary, 2015
Czerwonak, Poland

1978
Aleksander Holas

[p. 230]

Water Slide, 2008

Brooklyn, New York, NY, USA

1960
Morris Lapidus

Set in a brutalist open-air swimming pool designed by an architect whose name is usually associated with postwar Miami modern architecture, this concrete structure originally had metal slides attached. With their removal, the structure lost its function.
[p. 231]

Izbor Department Store, 2019

Bar, Montenegro

1984
Batrić Mijović

In stark contrast to Soviet state economy, Yugoslavia practiced a somewhat oxymoronic "market socialism", which ultimately proved very successful and resulted in a proliferation of shopping centres across the country, of which the Izbor Department Store is a prime. Its cluster of angular tent-shaped pavilion halls became one of Bar's distinctive features. [p. 232]

Okta Centrum, 2014

Former Rapla Kolkhoz,
Rapla, Estonia
1977
Toomas Rein

The Okta Centrum used to be the administrative and recreational building of the Rapla Kolkhoz. The octagonal shape is a motif used throughout the design, from the overall floor plan to the shape of columns, lamps and dustbins.
[p. 233]

Music Pavilion, 2006

Borjomi, Georgia

1982
S. Davitashvili, N. Solovyeva,
M. Zhuruli, G. Metonidze,
N. Karichashvili

The music pavillon is part of the House of Composers' Creative Work complex, set in the lush pine forest towering the spa city of Borjomi (see p. 202).
[p. 234]

Third Church of Christ, Scientist, 2012

Washington, DC, USA

1971
Araldo Cossutta (I.M. Pei & Partners)

The building, considered unsatisfactory by members of the Church's congregation, was destroyed in 2014. [p. 235]

285

House of Culture Auditorium, 2015

Kibbutz Netzer Sereni, Israel

1970s
Shimshon Heller

[p. 236]

Ben-Gurion Heritage Institute, 2015

Midreshet Sde Boker, The Negev,
Israel
1976
Arye Sharon, Eldar Sharon

[p. 237]

National Palace of Culture, 2013

Sofia, Bulgaria

1981
Alexander Georgiev Barov,
Ivan Kanazirev

The National Palace of Culture, which was opened in 1981 to commemorate Bulgaria's 1,300th anniversary, is the largest multifunctional centre in south-eastern Europe.
[p. 238]

Interfaith Medical Center, 2008

Brooklyn, New York, NY, USA

c. 1972
architect unknown

The Interfaith Medical Center resulted from the merge, in 1982, of Saint John's Episcopal Hospital and the Jewish Hospital and Medical Center. [p. 239]

General Secretariat of the Andean Community, 2018
Lima, Peru

1975
Arana Orrego Torres

The Andean Community is a free-trade area aiming at creating a customs union comprising the South American countries of Bolivia, Colombia, Ecuador and Peru.
[p. 240]

High Court of Australia, 2018
Canberra, Australia

1980
Christopher Kringas, Feiko Bouman and Rod Lawrence

This late modernist structure houses the highest court in the Australian judicial system. Its monumentality and sturdiness, associated with the extensive use of glass on the facade, are supposed to reflect the firmness of democracy as well as the transparency of its day-to-day function.
[p. 241]

Rugelis Holiday Complex, 2014
Palanga, Lithuania

1990
Saulius Šarkinas

The Rugelis Holiday Complex is one of the hotels of Vanagupé, the satellite city of the resort town of Palanga. It is built just opposite the Lino Swimming Pool (see p. 222).
[p. 242]

Lyndon B. Johnson Presidential Library and Museum, 2013
Austin, Texas, USA

1971
Gordon Bunshaft of Skidmore, Owings & Merrill

The Presidential Libraries are research centres and museums created to house the documents and artefacts of a given presidency. Most have a life-size replica of the Oval Office. Such is the case for the Johnson library whose replica, originally instated on the insistence of LBJ, was eventually placed on the top floor of the building.
[p. 243]

286

Niavaran Palace Library, 2015
Tehran, Iran

1977
Aziz Farmanfarmayan

Situated next to the historic Niavaran Palace, the library houses the private collection of Queen Farah Pahlavi. The collection contains over 23,000 volumes and over 350 artworks.
[p. 244]

Friends Club and Library, 2014
Kibbutz Gazit, Israel

1968
Hilik Arad

[p. 245]

Tel Hazor Archaeological Museum, 2015
Kibbutz Ayelet HaShahar, Israel

1964
David Resnick

A landmark of this kibbutz, this museum houses artefacts discovered in the 1950s on the site of Hazor, a Canaanite city from the 9th century BC, and mentioned in the biblical book of Joshua. Sadly, the museum faces financial problems due to the declining interest in archaeology, the ravages of earthquakes and inadequate maintenance. [p. 246]

Fish Market Canopy, 2018
Essaouira, Morocco

1980s
architect unknown

A late example of modernist design, with its cantilevered latticed roof adorned with multicoloured glass, this canopy was unfortunately poorly built and is threatened to be demolished.
[p. 247]

Gas Station, 2019

Ljubljana, Slovenia

1969
Edvard Ravnikar

This mushroom-shaped gas station is one of four structures commissioned by the Petrol oil company in Ljubljana. This design is probably the most ambitious, with three umbrellas spanning over 60 metres, but all stations make use of cantilevered roofs, the gravity-defying canopy resulting from modern technology and a metaphor for future living. [p. 248]

Canopy, 2018

Olympic Village, Munich, Germany

1972
Werner Wirsing

This sleek structure stands in the middle of the Munich Olympic Village, often described as "a city within a city". It was there that the infamous "Munich Massacre" took place, during which eleven Israeli Olympic sportsmen lost their lives after being kidnapped.
[p. 249]

Coffee Shop, 2010

International Fairgrounds, Tripoli, Lebanon
1975 (unfinished)
Oscar Niemeyer

[p. 250]

Canopy, 2012

Donbass Sanatorium, Massandra, Crimea, Russia
1964
Anatoly Polyansky, V.A. Somov

[p. 251]

Canopy, 2005

Artek Young Pioneers Camp, Hurzuf, Crimea, Russia
1964
Anatoly Polyansky

Artek was considered the most prestigious holiday camp for children in the Soviet Union and other communist countries. During its heyday, 27,000 children would vacation here every year. After 1991, its reputation declined and much of its infrastructure – including a sports stadium, swimming pools and a parade plaza overlooking the sea – fell into disrepair. [p. 252]

Bus Stop, 2012

Vinohradnyi, Crimea, Russia

1970s
architect unknown

[p. 253]

Bus Stop, 2012

Tulove, Crimea, Russia

1970s
architect unknown

[p. 254]

See first index entry, on p. 258.

MODERN FORMS

An Expanded Subjective Atlas of 20th-Century Architecture
Nicolas Grospierre

© Prestel Verlag, Munich · London · New York
A member of Penguin Random House Verlagsgruppe GmbH
Neumarkter Straße 28, 81673 Munich

© for the images, Nicolas Grospierre, 2022
© for the texts, the individual authors, 2022

Nicolas Grospierre wishes to thank: Agnieszka Rasmus-Zgorzelska, Aleksandra Stępnikowska, Grzegorz Piątek, Nika Grabar, Gunia Nowik, Bogna Świątkowska, Mart Kalm, Maija Rudovska, David Crowley, Paulina Latham, Ewa Łączyńska-Widz, Michael Jacobson, Julija Reklaitė, Amirali Ghasemi, Ana Chorgolashvili, James Pike, Ievgeniia Gubkina, Zvi Efrat, Yuval Yasky, Galia Bar Or, Irina Tchesnokova, Christopher Herwig, Piyumika Perera, Sharmini Pereira, Michelle Swatek, George Arbid, Asta Vaiciulyte, Karla Osorio, Bethe Beem, Maria Lanko, Mark Lamster, Iker Gil, Lee Bey, Mimi Zeiger, Alan Hess, Zbigniew Sielecki, Joanna Warsza, Aleksander Bykov, Hector Abarca, Antika Sawadsri, Salima Elmandjra, Henri Herré, Vents Vīnberg, Lahbib el Moumni, Slavica Stamatović Vuković, Evgeny Bereznitsky, Rosanna del Solar, Barbara Banaś, Martin Zaicek, Piotr Oszczanowski, Małgorzata Santarek, Daria Kravchuk.

The author wishes to extend his particular thanks to Alona Pardo, Elias Redstone and Lincoln Dexter, who edited the original edition of this book.

The images photographed in Estonia, Latvia, Lithuania and Israel in 2014 and 2015 were taken as part of a research project funded through a grant from the Graham Foundation for Advanced Studies in the Fine Arts. The image on p. 172 was achieved with the permission of the Eames Foundation.

Expanded edition first published in 2022

A CIP catalogue record for this book is available from the British Library.
Library of Congress Control Number: 2021044363

In respect to links in the book, the Publisher expressly notes that no illegal content was discernible on the linked sites at the time the links were created. The Publisher has no influence at all over the current and future design, content or authorship of the linked sites. For this reason the Publisher expressly disassociates itself from all content on linked sites that has been altered since the link was created and assumes no liability for such content.

Editorial direction: Anna Godfrey
Copy editor: Kim Scott
Layout and graphic design: Magdalena Ponagajbo
Research: Natalia Cichowska
Translation: Martyna Trykozko
Production: Corinna Pickart
Origination: Reproline Mediateam, Munich
Printing and binding: DZS Grafik d.o.o.
Paper: Magno Volume

FSC
MIX
Paper from responsible sources
FSC® C106600
www.fsc.org

Penguin Random House Verlagsgruppe FSC® N001967

Printed in Slovenia

ISBN 978-3-7913-8810-6

www.prestel.com